A E Lemmon
(1889-1963)
Artist and Craftsman

Frontispiece: A E Lemmon, working on a stained glass window for Taradale, New Zealand, 1955 (Photograph: Worcester Records Office).

A E Lemmon (1889-1963) Artist and Craftsman

The Stained Glass Windows
and other art works
of a Midlands Craftsman

Roy Albutt

Published in 2008 by Roy Albutt
11, Great Calcroft, Pershore, Worcestershire. WR10 1QS

Text copyright © Roy Albutt
Photographs © Roy Albutt

All rights reserved. No part of this publication
may be reproduced, stored in a retrieval system,
or transmitted in any form or by any means,
electronic, mechanical, photocopying, recording,
or otherwise, without written permission
of the publisher

ISBN 978-0-9543566-2-0

By the same author

Stained Glass windows of Bromsgrove and Redditch, Worcestershire (2002)

The Stained Glass Windows of A J Davies of the Bromsgrove Guild Worcestershire (2005)

Printed by
Warwick Printing Company Ltd, Caswell Road, Leamington Spa, Warwickshire, CV31 1QD

I have filled him with divine spirit, making him skilful and ingenious in every craft, and a master of design. Exodus 31.3

To the memory of my father,
Leslie John Albutt (1913-1974),
Craftsman and Teacher.

A E Lemmon Artist and Craftsman

Contents

List of Plates viii

Acknowledgements... x

Brief Biographical Details xi

1. Introduction 1
2. Education and Training... 4
3. Bromsgrove Guild and First World War Service 9
4. A E Lemmon – Artist and Craftsman 14
5. Commissions 20
6. Conclusion 39

Gazetteer of Stained Glass Windows 67

Gazetteer of Decorative Art Works... 81

Bibliography 91

Index 93

List of Plates

Cover: Bromsgrove, All Saints, *St Mary and St George* (detail), 1927.

Frontispiece: A E Lemmon, working on a stained glass window for Taradale, New Zealand, 1955 (Photograph: Worcestershire County Records Office). … … … … … … … ii

1. **National Medal for Success in Art awarded by the Board of Education** to Albert Lemmon as a student at the Birmingham School of Art. The inscription along the edge reads *Albert E Lemmon Design for Stained Glass, 1907.* … … … … … … 40

2. **St Valentine's Day Card,** by Albert Lemmon, sent to Hilda Bridgman in 1914. Albert and Hilda were married on 1 January 1918. … … 41

3. *Yuletide Greetings* **(1919)** cover of book of drawings by Albert Lemmon while he was on active service with the Cameron Highlanders in the First World War. … … … … … … … 42

4. *Yuletide Greetings*, p. 11, **New Year 1918**. … … … … 43

5. **Bromsgrove,** All Saints, *Annunciation and St George*, 1927, (detail). … 44

6. **Bromsgrove,** All Saints, *Annunciation and St George,* 1927, cartoon (detail). … … … … … … … … 45

7. **Bromsgrove,** All Saints, Church Warden's Stave, 1931. … … 46

8. **West Bromwich,** Christ Church (demolished), design for *St Aiden, St Augustine and St Chad*, 1928. … … … … … 47

9. **West Bromwich, Greets Green,** St Peter, *Te Deum*, 1930. … … 48

10. **Halesowen,** St Margaret, *Christ with Saints*, 1935. … … … 49

11. **Silian,** St Sulian, *Christ, St Mary and St David*, 1936, (detail). … 50

12. **Helpringham,** St Andrew, *Christ, St Hugh and St Andrew,* 1940. ... 51

13. **Helpringham,** St Andrew, Reredos, *Resurrection,* 1940. ... 52

14. **Thornborough,** St Mary, *Christ in Joseph's Workshop,* 1944. ... 53

15. **Thornborough,** St Mary, Rood Screen, 1946. ... 54

16. **Quadring,** St Margaret, *Christ in Majesty (The Seasons),* 1945. ... 55

17. **Wrangle,** St Mary and St Nicholas, *The Incarnation, St Hugh and St Nicholas,* 1949, design. ... 56

18. **Wrangle,** St Mary and St Nicholas, *The Incarnation, St Hugh and St Nicholas* 1949, detail of cartoon. ... 57

19. **Wrangle,** St Mary and St Nicholas, *The Incarnation, St Hugh and St Nicholas,* 1949. ... 58

20. **Sedgley, Dudley,** St Mary, *St Christopher,* 1949. ... 59

21. **Lye, Stourbridge,** Christ Church, *World War II Memorial,* 1951. ... 60

22. **Evesham, Bengeworth,** St Peter, *Eoves' Vision,* 1954. ... 61

23. **Bromsgrove,** St John, *Boy Scout,* 1958 (detail). ... 62

24. **Taradale, New Zealand,** All Saints, cartoon for *Trinity* window, 1956, (detail). ... 63

25. **Bromsgrove, Catshill,** Christ Church, *St Chad,* 1958. ... 64

26. **Altar Cross,** Gesso, paint and gold leaf on wood, date unknown, privately owned. ... 65

27. **Portrait of Peter Lemmon,** enamel, 1926, privately owned. ... 66

Acknowledgements

The late Peter Lemmon, Albert's son, in correspondence over a six-year period, provided insights into the life, family and work of his father. Talking with Alan Meredith gave me invaluable information into the work of the Lemmon studio, for which I am most grateful.

I am indebted to Neil Phillips of the John Hardman & Co. Ltd, Stained Glass Studios who gave me unlimited access to their Lemmon archive of cartoons, designs and photograph album, and permitted me to take photographs, some of which are reproduced in this book. (Plates 6, 8, 17, 18 and 24).

Sian Everett, Archivist at Birmingham Institute of Art and Design (formerly Birmingham School of Art) was most helpful in allowing me to consult records relating to Lemmon's training at the Birmingham School of Art. Liet Col (Retired) A M Cummings OBE, Regimental Headquarters the Highlanders, Inverness, kindly provided information concerning Lemmon's service with the Cameron Highlanders.

I am grateful to Mr M G Huskinson, Registrar of Worcester Diocese, Mr H B Carslake, Registrar of Birmingham Diocese and Mr D M Wellman, Registrar of Lincoln Diocese for allowing me to consult faculties. Mr Tim Clayton, Secretary to DAC, Birmingham Diocese, was most helpful.

My thanks go to the staff at Worcester Records Office, Worcester Family History Centre, Lichfield Records Office, Dudley Archives and Lincolnshire Archives. Librarians at Birmingham Central Library and Archive, and Worcestershire Library Service, were most helpful. The Revd Gerald Clarke kindly sent me details of the two Lemmon windows at All Saints Church, Taradale, New Zealand.

I would like to thank John Bridgman, Alan Brooks, Brian Franks, Sue Lauzier, Archivist of the Worcestershire Guild of Designer Craftsmen, Mike Wilks, Mrs B G Sanders and Bromsgrove Museum. I also thank my wife Joan for her continued patience and encouragement during my research into stained glass windows.

I wish to thank Worcestershire County Records Office for permission to reproduce the photograph of A E Lemmon working on a stained glass window (frontispiece). The remaining photographs are my own.

Finally, I acknowledge the help of the Clergy, Church Wardens, and members of the congregations of the churches I have visited in order to record and photograph Lemmon windows and other art works. Without their kind cooperation, my research would not have been possible.

A E Lemmon – A Brief Biography

1889	Born, 84, Great Tindale Street, Ladywood, Birmingham, on 29 September.
1903	Commenced Evening Classes at Birmingham School of Art, on 8 September.
1903	Began full-time at Birmingham School of Art, on 1 December.
1904-08	Awarded prizes, National and local, for student work at Birmingham School of Art.
1908	Completed course at Birmingham School of Art.
1909	Joined the Stephen Adam Studio, Glasgow, under Alfred Webster.
c. 1911	Joined the A J Davies Studio at the Bromsgrove Guild, Bromsgrove, Worcestershire.
1915	Enlisted in The Queen's Own Cameron Highlanders, on 29 May.
1918	Married Hilda (b 24 Dec 1892), daughter of Jabez Bridgman, Townsend Mill, Bromsgrove, on 1 January.
1919	Returned to the A J Davies studio at the Bromsgrove Guild on demobilisation.
1920	Peter Edward Lemmon born.
1927	Left the A J Davies studio at the Bromsgrove Guild to set up on his own.
1929	Appointed Art Teacher at Bromsgrove Art School, in July, a post he held until the 1950s.
1939-45	Member of Bromsgrove Home Guard during World War II.
1953	Founder member of the Worcestershire Guild of Designer Craftsmen.
1963	A E Lemmon died on 4 February, aged 73 years.
2004	Death of P E Lemmon on 27 March aged 83.

1. Introduction

Albert Lemmon's name was familiar to me when I was in my early teens growing up in Bromsgrove. His name came up in conversations between my paternal grandfather and my father and uncle. T H Albutt & Son (my uncle was the son) was a Bromsgrove plastering and general building company. The context (I realised many years later) was probably because Lemmon supplied leaded lights for building work undertaken by my grandfather. It may also have been because of a common avid interest in the local football team, Bromsgrove Rovers!

I became aware of Albert Lemmon as a designer and maker of stained glass windows while researching the A J Davies stained glass studio at the celebrated Bromsgrove Guild.[1] I began to record and photograph Lemmon windows and wrote to his son Peter, who still lived in the Lemmon family home in Bromsgrove, in January 1998. In his reply to my letter Peter wrote that he had known a Leslie Albutt, a woodwork teacher – this was my late father. Albert Lemmon and my father had been colleagues at Bromsgrove College of Further Education c. 1950. I sent details of his father and his family, taken from the 1901 census, as well as photographs of Lemmon windows to Peter. He responded by looking out family photographs, greetings cards and other material which he sent to me. These I photographed and returned. Thirty-eight letters passed between us. I finally met Peter at his home on 16 February 2004. His last letter to me, dated 4 March, arrived shortly before his death on 27 March 2004, aged 83. Peter's letters provided insights into the life, family and work of Albert Lemmon.

Another important source of information is the Lemmon Archive at John Hardman Studios. Peter removed the contents of the studio when Albert died and gave stained glass window cartoons, a number of watercolour designs, an album of photographs of windows and other art works taken by Albert and Peter, and a few tools including a badger brush, to the Hardman Studio. Peter gave the material to the Hardman Studios since he felt that the long-term future of the Bromsgrove Museum was somewhat precarious. At the Hardman Stained Glass Studio, I was able to photograph the archive material. Many of the cartoons I recognised from windows I had already seen, other were labelled and this was invaluable in locating other churches with works by Lemmon, although some had been demolished. The photograph album was informative yet frustrating. It led me to additional windows and other works but also emphasised the loss (or at best unknown whereabouts) of some of Lemmon's output, especially from decommissioned churches in the West Midlands conurbation.

I was fortunate to become acquainted with Alan Meredith of Bromsgrove who worked with Albert Lemmon from 1947 to 1950. Alan was a student in Albert Lemmon's art classes before being employed in his High Street studio. Alan was able to talk about the layout of the studio and working practices. I have visited the building that housed the studio. The rooms are now in use as offices.

An unexpected source of Lemmon's leaded light designs came from John Thompson, a stained glass worker, who lives in Hamilton, Victoria, Australia. John acquired a copy of a catalogue of a stained glass maker based at Lye in Stourbridge in the West Midlands, which contained loose copies of designs by Lemmon. One of the designs has Lemmon's name and address written on it in Lemmon's hand and another is stamped with a Bromsgrove building company hand-stamp.

I set out to record and photograph only the stained glass windows of A E Lemmon but soon became aware of the many other art works which he produced and extended my research to include these. What appeared initially to be a relatively straightforward piece of research into a small number of stained glass windows has proved to be a lengthier and more exciting exercise than I had anticipated.

As my research progressed, it became apparent to me that Albert Lemmon's life revolved around two themes. These were his family and his art. This included not only his immediate family, wife Hilda and son Peter, but also his extended family of brothers and sisters. Peter sent me Birthday and Valentine cards, which Albert had made and sent to Hilda before they were married some ninety years before. These had been treasured and kept in the family home, as had a photograph of the Lemmon family probably taken when Albert was only one. Albert's father was a carpenter. I believe that Albert, when painting on glass or wood, scenes depicting Christ in His father's workshop, used his father's face for Joseph. When Albert enlisted in the army in 1915, he joined the Cameron Highlanders, presumably because his brother William served with that regiment. William had been an apprentice carpenter but joined the army after a row with his father. As a child, Peter recalled making regular visits with his parents to 84, Great Tindal Street, Ladywood, Birmingham, where Albert had been born, to visit Aunt Elizabeth. Another of Albert's sisters, Anne (known to Peter as Aunt Nance), married Frederick Frost, a Catholic, and they moved to Bromsgrove where they had a house built. Albert made leaded lights for the property. He also used the garage when he needed a large convenient space to work in (his studio in Bromsgrove was on the first floor, up narrow stairs). A stained glass window was designed and made at the studio in memory of Albert's other brother, George Frank, who emigrated to New

Zealand. Peter was still corresponding with his elderly cousins in New Zealand in 2002. Peter's image appeared in artwork by his father, for example, the Annunciation window at All Saints Church, Bromsgrove, and a small enamel portrait of Peter aged seven. The inclusion of Peter's signature on windows and painted panels displays Albert's desire to include his son in his artistic output, even where Peter's contribution was suspiciously small. Close contact with family, his own and his wife's, was such an important aspect of Albert's life.

The second, all-absorbing aspect of Albert Lemmon's life was his artwork. In the design and making of stained glass windows, painted panels, reredoses, altarpieces, candlesticks, banners and enamels, and teaching post at Bromsgrove School of Art, Albert was dedicated to using his considerable artistic abilities. Albert's watercolour designs, for individual stained glass windows or the refurbishment of an entire chapel in a Lincolnshire church, are works of art in their own right. His cartoons for stained glass windows are very detailed, with almost every brush-stroke being included. Peter wrote that his father 'spent too much time on working drawings. It was my mother's and my opinion that was why every job was a financial mess. It was impossible to change him'.

Albert Lemmon seems to have led a contented life in Bromsgrove. He moved to the town around 1911. He spent what must have been four harrowing years in the trenches during the First World War, even then he continued to sketch and paint. Following his marriage to a local girl, they settled in Bromsgrove and spent the rest of their lives together living in a terraced house a short walk from the town centre.

In documenting the life and work of this artist and craftsman, I am aware that my research is incomplete and I would be pleased to hear from anyone who knows the location of additional works, including any mentioned in my gazetteer, which may have been moved from decommissioned or demolished churches.

Albert Lemmon's memorial is to be found in five churches in the Bromsgrove area which contain his work, none more so than All Saints Church where he and Hilda were married and where they worshipped.[2]

---

[1] For information on A J Davies see Albutt, Roy, *The Stained Glass Windows of A J Davies of the Bromsgrove Guild* (2005), for the Bromsgrove Guild see Watt, Quentin, (Ed), *The Bromsgrove Guild An Illustrated History* (1999).

[2] In addition to All Saints Church, there are windows and other works at St Peter's RC Church, St Godwold's Church, Finstall, Christ Church, Catshill, Bromsgrove Methodist Church, and St John's Church, Bromsgrove.

2. Education and Training

Albert Edward Lemmon was born on 29 September 1889. He was the youngest of the six children of William and Sarah (nee Hodgetts) Lemmon[1]. William Lemmon, born 31 March 1844 at Newbold Verdon, Leicestershire, was a carpenter and joiner like his father before him. Sarah, who was born in 1843, was the daughter of a bricklayer and came from Tipton in Staffordshire. William and Sarah were married in 1873 in Leicester, where their two eldest children were born, and later moved to Birmingham. The family was living at 84, Great Tindal Street, Ladywood, when Albert was born, and in 1905 moved to nearby Alston Street.

Ladywood, Birmingham

Birmingham experienced an enormous increase in population in the nineteenth century as the result of an expansion in manufacturing industries. This in turn led to unplanned urban growth of densely packed terraced housing to accommodate workers and their families. Ladywood, part of the inner city, developed in the 1850s with the construction of cheaply built back-to-back housing. Such housing was often crowded and unsanitary, as well as being close to manufacturing premises where the population found work. It was to Ladywood that the Lemmon family moved from Leicester in about 1873, presumably to improved working opportunities for William Lemmon. Living first in Great Tindal Street, the family later moved the short distance to Alston Street. Albert's eldest sister, Elizabeth, retained the tenancy of the house in Great Tindal Street. Peter Lemmon visited his Aunt Bess (Elizabeth) as a child, recalling 'street after street of back-to-back houses built for the industrial revolution. One loo in the yard for about three houses'.[2]

In 1903, at the age of thirteen, Albert Lemmon enrolled for a full-time course at the Birmingham Municipal School of Art where the records show that he gave 'Stained Glass Worker' as his proposed occupation. Why would a thirteen year old from Ladywood aspire to become a stained glass worker?

There existed a tradition of stained glass window making in the Birmingham area at this time, so it is could be that he was influenced by friends or neighbours who worked at one of the local firms. The premises of stained glass makers William Pearce and Swaine Bourne were located less than half a mile from his Tindal Street home. The well-known companies John Hardman & Co and Jones and Willis were located near to the centre of the city and within three miles to the west, at Smethwick, T W Camm, Camm & Co. and Samuel Evans were all producing stained glass windows.[3]

The stained glass windows in the city's two main churches may also have influenced Albert Lemmon with their exceptional examples of the art of stained glass making. St Chad's Roman Catholic Cathedral has impressive windows mainly by John Hardman, while St Philip's Church (which became the Anglican Cathedral when Birmingham became a city in 1905) has the stunning Morris & Co. windows designed for his hometown by Edward Burne-Jones.

It is likely that the Lemmon family attended the nearby church of St Margaret of Antioch which had stained glass windows by Samuel Evans.[4] St Margaret's Church was consecrated in 1875 and seated 740. It was made redundant in 1956 and demolished. It is interesting to note that on 8 November 1911 a faculty was approved for a design by Albert Lemmon for a window for St Margaret's Church depicting *Christ Blessing Children* in memory of the Reverend Arthur Orlando Cherrington.[5] The present location of the window is not known or even whether it survived the demolition.

Albert Lemmon must have received the encouragement and support of his teachers at the nearby St John's Church of England School, which he attended. Presumably he showed an aptitude for drawing which, together with a recommendation from his head teacher, would have been the deciding factor in securing his place at the School of Art.

Albert received encouragement from his parents, and his brothers and sisters, in applying for a place at the School of Art. The four eldest Lemmon children had probably begun work as soon as they reached school leaving age by entering trades. The occupations of Elizabeth and Ellen are given as 'stay and corset maker' in the 1891 census. William, the eldest son, became a carpenter like his father but following an argument with his father, he left home to join the army.[6] He joined the Cameron Highlanders in January 1892, eventually becoming Regimental Sergeant Major in the Royal Warwickshire Regiment. George, the second of the Lemmon boys, emigrated to New Zealand where a window, designed and made by Albert, was erected in his memory in 1956 (see gazetteer). The two youngest children, Ann and Albert, entered professions. Anne became a schoolteacher while Albert, an artist–craftsman, was also qualified to teach art and craft, after completing his course at the School of Art.

Proud parents must have watched thirteen-year-old Albert set out to begin his course at Birmingham Municipal School of Art less than a mile away in the centre of the city.

Birmingham School of Art

Birmingham School of Art originated in 1847 as the Birmingham Government School of Design. In 1885 it moved to new purpose-built premises in Margaret

Street, Birmingham as the Municipal School of Art, called the Central School to distinguish it from the many Branch Schools established in the suburbs of the city.[7] In 1892, due to the efforts of the head teacher Edward R Taylor, the building was extended and reorganised into 'practical craft workshops, re-titled Art Laboratories'.[8] This allowed students to execute their designs in a variety of crafts including modelling and casting, enamelling, foundry work and woodcarving as well as undertaking cartoons, fresco, tempera and other painting. Designing stained glass windows had been part of the curriculum for some time but the actual making of stained glass windows did not begin until 1901.

The ethos of the Central School was firmly based in the Arts and Crafts Movement. Pevsner called it the 'first conceived under the influence of the Morris movement'.[9] William Morris and Edward Burne-Jones served as Honorary Presidents of the School of Art in the 1870s and 1880s.

The curriculum followed by students was the National Course of Study which consisted of a series of progressive stages beginning with drawing and shading from objects leading to the drawing of plants, animals and the human figure from casts and life. The next stage consisted of a similar course in painting in different media. The final stages involved modelling and drawing, including moulding and casting, lithography, wood carving, porcelain painting and the design and making of stained glass windows.

In 1901, the headmaster sent Henry Payne, a young teacher who had trained as a student at the School of Art, to learn the craft of stained glass making under Christopher Whall at Lowndes and Drury Stained Glass Studios in London. Payne proved to be an able student of the Arts and Crafts stained glass maker and teacher Whall. In a letter to the Management Committee of the School of Art Whall wrote that he was 'more than satisfied with Mr Payne's performance during the three months'. On his return to Birmingham Payne established a stained glass department at the School of Art.

Albert Lemmon began his time as a student at the Central School of Art on September 8th 1903 when he attended evening classes. That same year he was soon enrolled as a free admission on the full-time advanced course. During each of his five years at the School of Art Lemmon was to receive a scholarship. School of Art records show that he was a Kenrick Scholar in 1904 and received a Ryland Scholarship in 1906.[10]

Lemmon is mentioned on a number of occasions in the Prize Lists which were published by the School of Art to record the successes of students in Local and National competitions. In 1905 he received twelve shillings (60 pence) as third prize for Original Drawing and Work in Stained Glass. In 1906 he was awarded a 2nd Class in Drawing of Common Objects from Memory by the Government

Department of Science and Art. In the following year, 1907, he was awarded 1st Class Honours in the Design Awards by the Department of Science and Art. Perhaps the most pleasing of Lemmon's awards was the 'National Medal for Success in Art Awarded by the Board of Education'. The edge of the medal bears the inscription 'Albert E Lemmon Design for Stained Glass, 1907'. This bronze medal is still in the possession of Lemmon's descendants (Plate 1).

While training at the School of Art Lemmon met fellow students who were to become established as stained glass artists. Richard Stubington (1885-1966) took over the teaching of stained glass when Payne left in 1909. A J Davies (1877-1953), like many other students finished his course and then taught at Branch Schools while continuing to train at the Central School. Davies established his studio in premises at the Bromsgrove Guild in 1906.[11] Joseph Newbould Sanders (1885-1933) and Henry George Rushbury (1889-1968), also trained at Birmingham, later joined the Davies' studio at Bromsgrove as assistants. Another student at the School of Art was Florence Camm, who worked with her brothers at the firm of Thomas William Camm established by her father in 1868. Albert Lemmon would have known Davies, Sanders, Rushbury and Florence Camm as fellow students.

The course in stained glass making offered at the Birmingham School of Art by Payne from 1901 to 1909, when he left to establish a studio in the Cotswolds, and continued by Stubington, was an important one for the training of stained glass artists in the Midlands.

Glasgow

Soon after completing his course at the Birmingham School of Art, in the summer of 1908, Albert Lemmon moved to Glasgow to work for Alf Webster in the Stephen Adam Studio according to a report of his death in the local paper, based presumably on information provided by Lemmon's wife and son Peter.[12]

I have been unsuccessful in my search for documentary evidence in Scotland to confirm that Lemmon worked at the Stephen Adam Studio.[13] Working with Alf Webster would have provided an ideal opportunity for Albert Lemmon to become a member of a successful stained glass studio after graduating from the School of Art.

Alfred Alexander Webster (1884-1915) joined Stephen Adam (1884-1910) in his Glasgow studio in 1904. In 1909, he became a junior partner and on the death of Stephen Adam in 1910 took over the studio.[14] The studio would have been under the direction of Alf Webster by 1909, when Lemmon probably began working there. The Adam Studio at this time produced some remarkable windows including a number at New Kilpatrick Parish Church and later at Lansdowne Church in Glasgow.[15] Lemmon may well have been working for Alf Webster when *The First*

Fruits window, 'the small but very beautiful memorial lancet', was dedicated to Stephen Adam, at New Kilpatrick Parish Church, in 1911.

In March 1915, by which time Lemmon was working at Bromsgrove in the Davies stained glass studio, Alf Webster joined the Gordon Highlanders. Webster served in France where he died of war wounds on 24 August 1915. Albert Lemmon kept a photograph, apparently cut from a newspaper, of '2/Lieut. Alf A Webster'.[16]

---

1   The Lemmon children were Elizabeth born 1870, William Henry (1872), Frances Ellen (1874), George Frank (1876), Anne Isabel (1879) and Albert Edward (1889).
2   Letter to author dated 20 May 2002.
3   The 1900 edition of Kelly's Directory of Birmingham lists nine Glass Painters, including William Pearce in Bridge Street, Birmingham, and T W Camm, Camm & Co. and Samuel Evans all at Smethwick. There were 10 Glass Stainers and Quickers, including Swaine Bourne, King Edward Road, and Jones and Willis, Edmund Street. John Hardman & Co. of Newhall Street was listed under Glass Decorators.
4   Worcester Diocese Calendar for 1900, when Birmingham was still part of that diocese, has an advertisement by Samuel Evans & Son which lists a number of churches with windows by the firm, including 'St Margaret's, Birmingham (3)'.
5   Birmingham Diocese Records include a design sketch for this window – see gazetteer.
6   Peter Lemmon mentioned an argument, which William had with his father, in a letter to the author dated 20 May 2002.
7   In 1903 when Albert Lemmon began his course of study there were 11 Branch Schools.
8   Swift, 1996, p. 13.
9   Pevsner, 1937, p. 139.
10 William Kenrick, a member of a family of hardware manufacturers, was a Birmingham Councillor, an Alderman and an MP. He was also Chairman of the School of Art management Committee. (Hartnell, pp. 55-56). Louisa Anne Ryland, as well as giving scholarships, had donated £10,000 towards building the School of Art in Margaret Street, as did Richard Tangye. The land on which it was built was given by Cregoe Coleman (Hartnell, p. 74).
11 For details of Davies' career see Albutt, 2005.
12 Bromsgrove Artist Died At Fireside', in Bromsgrove Messenger, 8 February 1963.
13 My thanks to the staff of Libraries and to the Art Historians I contacted in Scotland in my attempts to find documentary evidence for the time Albert Lemmon spent north of the border.
14 Honey, p.1.
15 Windows at New Kilpatrick Parish Church, Bearsden, by the Adams Studio include the Henderson Memorial of 1910, *The First Fruits*, 1911, *The Gift of Life* window and *Prayer and Praise*. See McCardel (1973) and Donnelly (1997).
    Donelly (1997) considers the north and south transept windows of 1913 in Lansdowne Church, Glasgow, by Alf Webster, to be among 'the crowning achievements of Scottish stained glass'. My thanks to Jack Stuart for enabling me to see these windows.
16 See Chapter 4, Cameron Highlanders.

3. The Bromsgrove Guild

Albert Lemmon was an assistant to A J Davies in his studio at the Bromsgrove Guild until 1927, except for a break for war service.

The Bromsgrove Guild of Applied Arts was established in 1898 by Walter Gilbert (1871-1946) the head teacher of Bromsgrove School of Art. Gilbert, originally from Rugby, had trained at Birmingham School of Art, and held teaching posts in Rugby and Harrow before moving to Bromsgrove.[1] Gilbert, a charismatic person, obtained commissions for the Guild which were carried out by artists and craftsmen in studios and workshops based at Bromsgrove, Birmingham and elsewhere. The Guild soon established a reputation when awarded medals for their exhibits in the British Pavilion at the Paris Exhibition of 1900. By 1903 workshops and studios had been established at Bromsgrove for metalwork casting, leadwork, plaster, jewellery and enamels with further workshops and studios in Birmingham producing stoneworking, furniture, stained glass and embroideries[2] Many of the artists and craftsmen in Birmingham were staff at the Birmingham School of Art. Gilbert later attracted artists and craftsmen to enlarged Guild premises at Bromsgrove, many from the continent.

Gilbert continued to obtain commissions at home and abroad including many for stained glass windows. Stained glass work had been undertaken by Henry Payne (1868-1940), Mary Newill (1860-1947) and Bernard Sleigh (1872-1954) at the Birmingham School of Art but with their teaching commitments and their own commissions they were unable or unwilling to undertake the work. Gilbert was anxious to establish a studio at Bromsgrove and in 1906 Archibald John Davies (1877-1953), a student of Henry Payne, was invited to move to Bromsgrove to set up a stained glass department in Guild premises.

The studio Davies established was, in effect, his private studio. The paperwork for commissions was undertaken by Guild clerical staff but Davies retained overall responsibility. There were sufficient commissions, from home and abroad, for Davies to appoint assistants. Two of these, Joseph Sanders and Henry Rushbury had both been students of Henry Payne at the Birmingham School of Art and would have been known to Davies

When Lemmon moved to Bromsgrove Henry Rushbury had already left the studio but Lemmon worked alongside Joseph Sanders with whom he became friendly.[3] A portrait of Albert Lemmon painted on glass, still in the possession of his relatives, is the work of Joseph Sanders.[4]

Another member of the studio was Henry 'Harry' John Hodgetts (1897-1964), a stained glass cutter, leader and fitter who had moved from Birmingham to work in the Davies studio. Harry Hodgetts proved to be the longest serving member of the studio. When Davies died in 1953 he helped to complete and pack an unfinished commission for Halifax, Canada before the studio closed. Arthur Slade Clarke (1893-1993) began work as an apprentice with Davies in 1910 and remained with the studio until 1935.[5]

Lemmon's move to Bromsgrove to work at the Guild is likely to have been around 1911. In December 1912 he designed and made a card to celebrate the 20th birthday of a local young lady, Hilda Bridgman. On the card, Lemmon has written 'Wishing you many happy returns of the Day from A E Lemmon'. Perhaps this somewhat formal greeting indicates a recent acquaintance. The following year 'Bert' sent Hilda another card which he had made to celebrate her coming of age. The card he sent on 'Saint Valentine Day 1914' has a self-portrait of Albert Lemmon in Scottish dress on the front holding a heart-shaped cut-out. Visible through the cut-out, painted on the inside of the card, is a scene with Townsend Mill in the foreground and in the distance the spire of St John's Church Bromsgrove (Plate 2).

Hilda lived at the family mill, Townsend Mill, located about a kilometre out of the town on the road to Birmingham. Townsend Mill was a corn mill driven by the waters of Spadesbourne Brook. The Bridgman family acquired the mill in 1873 and made a living grinding grain for animal feed. The mill remained in the family until the 1950s.[6]

Work at the Bromsgrove Guild and courting of Hilda Bridgman was interrupted by the outbreak of the Great War. Albert Lemmon decided to enlist and fight for king and country. In 1915, he joined the Cameron Highlanders.

The First World War – Cameron Highlanders

On 28 May 1915, 'aged 25 years and 270 days' Albert Lemmon enlisted in The Queen's Own Cameron Highlanders.[7] He gave his occupation as 'artist'. He presumably chose to join the Cameron Highlanders because his eldest brother William Henry, by then 43 years of age, was a Sergeant in the Regiment.[8]

After initial training, Private Lemmon, Number 184345, was posted to France on 1 October 1915 to join the Fifth Battalion the Cameron Highlanders. He served in France and Belgium with this Regiment for the duration of the War. While on active service in Europe Lemmon produced a remarkable pictorial record of the conditions endured by the soldiers in his regiment (Plates 3 and 4). He carried with him his box of watercolours, pencils and paper to record scenes of battles, the capturing of enemy soldiers, the wounded, war-damaged buildings, extracts of poetry and even a New Year concert party. In 1919 his work was published as *Yuletide Greetings from the 5th Battalion Cameron Highlanders*, a collection of thirteen black and white images, 9 cm wide by 13 cm high, each a compilation of named and dated scenes showing the awful conditions of life in the trenches on the battlefields of north-eastern France from May 1915 to 1919. Familiar names associated with First World War battles appearing in the publication include Ypres, the Somme and Passchendale. There are four introductory pages and a coloured cover page. The last page is dated 1919 and takes the form of a greetings card. Each page of illustrations, printed only on the right-hand page, is signed with the initials AEL, some within a shield. Lemmon later used the same device to sign his stained glass windows and other works. The final page bears a shield saying 'Designed in the field by Albert E Lemmon L/C'. By 1919, Private Lemmon had become Lance-Corporal Lemmon but more importantly, he had survived the war. He was demobilised on 15 May 1919.

Albert Lemmon's own copy of *Yuletide Greetings* has autographs of officers and men of the regiment. There are also a number of photographs cut from newspapers. These additions and annotations, some with dates of deaths, are on the blank left-hand pages. They were later additions, perhaps following regimental gatherings.[9]

It is interesting to note that opposite page three there is a head and shoulders photograph, beneath which Lemmon has written '2/Lieut. Alf. A. Webster 3rd Gordons Atted 1st Camerons Killed in Action August 24th 1915'.[10] Lemmon has also drawn an artists' palette and brushes resting on a ceremonial sword. I wonder whether Albert Lemmon's decision to join the army was influenced by the fact that Alf Webster had joined some two months before. Perhaps this is further evidence that Albert Lemmon was a studio assistant to Alf Webster at the Stephen Adam Studio, and a token of the respect and affection he felt for the fellow craftsman.

On the 1st January 1918 twenty-eight year old Albert Lemmon, on leave from war service in France, married Hilda Bridgman, aged 25, at All Saints Church, Bromsgrove. As wedding presents from the Bromsgrove Guild the couple received two cast circular, bronze-coloured metal plaques, ten centimetres in diameter, set in oak frames. The plaques depict a *Nativity* and *The Conversion of St Hubert*. These exquisite objects are probably the work of Louis Weingartner, a gifted Swiss art metalworker who collaborated with Walter Gilbert on many of the Guild's most notable commissions.[11]

Albert Lemmon was fortunate to survive the dreadful carnage of battles and conditions of life in the trenches. Like others who fought in France and Belgium, he was awarded the 1914-15 Star, the 1914-18 British War Medal and the Victory Medal.

Return to the Bromsgrove Guild

Albert Lemmon returned to the Davies studio after demobilisation from the Cameron Highlanders in May 1919. He now had a wife to support and in 1920 their only child, Peter Edward, was born at 45, Birmingham Road, a terraced house a short walk from Bromsgrove High Street. Albert and Hilda lived their entire married lives at number 45, Birmingham Road.

The First World War, with its dreadful loss of life, provided Guild artists and craftsmen with many commissions to commemorate those who lost their lives in the hostilities. As well as stained glass windows, memorials in wood, metal and stone were commissioned from Bromsgrove Guild workshops.

Lemon rejoined Davies and his assistants Arthur Clarke and 'Harry' Hodgetts in the ugly three-storey corrugated-iron buildings at the southern end of the town that housed the Guild craftsmen. The Davies stained glass studio occupied the two upper floors of the north building. Lemmon must have enjoyed the relative tranquillity of the studio in the small market town after his experiences in the trenches of war-torn Europe.

Soon after the War the Davies studio was engaged in designing and making war memorial windows. Lemmon would have vividly recalled his experiences on the battlefields of France and Belgium as he worked on windows to commemorate those who had failed to return. Some windows were erected as parish memorials with the names of the dead included in the inscription, others in memory of an individual serviceman. A *Holy Grail* window, a design characteristic of the studio, erected at Churchill, Worcestershire in 1920, is in memory of a 2nd Lieut., a Corporal, Lance Corporal and four Privates from the village. Another on the same theme, commemorating the life of Lieutenant A. Fisher Smith, is in St Peter's Church, Wolverhampton. Two more windows from the Bromsgrove studio, both of 1921, may display the hand of Albert Lemmon. A two light window in Belford Hostel (former Dean Free Church), Edinburgh, has three uniformed Scottish soldiers before a seated Virgin and Child. The soldiers, dressed in Scottish uniforms, are depicted in a design similar to the cover of *Yuletide Greetings,* with two standing and another kneeling. The 6th Battalion, The Prince of Wales Own West Yorkshire Regiment memorial window, in Bradford Cathedral, has battle scenes similar to, but less graphic, than those that Lemmon illustrated in his book on the Cameron Highlanders. Some battle names are, not surprisingly, the same in both window and book. The West Yorkshire Regiment and the Cameron Highlanders took part in battles at Ypes and Passchendaele.[12] I see Lemmon's hand in the battle scenes in this window.

Albert Lemmon seems to have worked happily with Davies on the many commissions for home and abroad that the studio attracted, until 1927. In that year, Lemmon left the Guild to establish his own studio in the town.

1. For detailed information on the Bromsgrove Guild, see Watt, Quintin, *The Bromsgrove Guild: An Illustrated History*, (1999).
2. Bromsgrove Guild advertisement in *The Connoisseur*, January 1903.
3. Conversation with Mrs B G Sanders, Joseph Sanders' daughter-in-law.
4. Joseph Sanders married Emily Gibbs, a Bromsgrove girl, in 1912. Later that year they moved to Lancaster where Sanders worked in the stained glass studios of Abbot & Co. Sanders later went into partnership with A Barrowclough. Barrowclough and Sanders studios were at Greaves, Lancaster.
5. Kings, Bill, *Old Rover: Selections from the Cartoons of Arthur Clarke*, (Bromsgrove: Silly Symbols productions, 1993).
6. Briggs, p. 80
7. Letter to author from Lieutenant Colonel (Retd) A M Cumming OBE, Regimental Headquarters, The Highlanders, Cameron Barracks, Inverness.
8. William Henry Lemmon later became Regimental Sergeant Major of the Royal Warwickshire Regiment.
9. Lemmon's copy of *Yuletide Greetings* has been handed down within the family.
10. Honey, Thomas M (2002) writes 'Alf Webster joined the Gordon Highlanders in March 1915, was posted to the front line and died of war wounds on 24th August 1915', Introduction.
11. Birmingham Museum and Art Gallery Sound Archive transcript, *Arthur Slade Clarke*, 1984, pp. 45-6.
12. Details of these windows may be found in Albutt, R., *The Stained Glass Windows of A J Davies of the Bromsgrove Guild Worcestershire*, 2005.

4. A E Lemmon 'Artist and Craftsman'[1]

Albert Lemmon left the Davies studio at the Bromsgrove Guild 'in 1927 after falling out with Davies'.[2] Initially he worked from his home at 45, Birmingham Road, Bromsgrove, a modest terraced house. The house was known as Holly Villa, a name still to be found in a semi-circular stained glass window over the door. He later rented a studio above a shop in Bromsgrove High Street.

From 1927 until his death in 1963, Albert Lemmon designed and made stained glass windows and a wide variety of ecclesiastical and other decorative items. He completed over sixty stained glass windows, and countless 'leaded lights'. The wide range of ecclesiastical decorative items included painted reredoses, altarpieces and other panels, altar crosses and candlesticks, riddel posts, painted carved angels, processional crosses, churchwardens' staves, painted wooden panels, painted banners and even a painted plaster statue of Our Lady (Plates 7, 13, 15, 26 and 27). Other art works included enamels, a dedicatory illuminated page, a series of drawings of regimental cap badges and a Christmas card designed while a member of the Home Guard during the Second World War.

Most of the painted wooden objects had details in gesso applied before the paint, which meant that certain parts, such as haloes, heraldry or inscriptions, could be given emphasis in low relief. Lemmon wrote that the gesso he used he made from 'whiting mixed with size obtained by boiling vellum and parchment'.[3]

Lemmon's painted altar crosses and candlesticks were mainly coloured using traditional heraldic colours of red (gules) and blue (azure) with the generous use of gold and silver leaf. The backs of crosses and candlesticks were often painted black, with gold or silver leaf, enabling them to be reversed during the celebration of Christ's passion at Easter.

The wooden 'blanks' for the reredoses, crosses, candlesticks and processional crosses were the work of the local firm of Pancheri and Hack of Aston Fields, Bromsgrove, a firm of wood and stone carvers. Celestino Pancheri, a wood carver from the Austrian Tyrol, joined the Bromsgrove Guild in 1908. In 1926 he left the Guild to establish Pancheri and Hack, wood and stone carvers of Bromsgrove. His son Robert continued the tradition of carving.[4]

Lemmon worked in the Davies studio for some ten years (excluding war service) yet there is no obvious comparison between the designs of the two studios. Faces depicted in Lemmon's windows are those of everyday people (Plates 9, 11, 18 and 21). Perhaps Davies painted the faces in Guild windows. Lemmon's work is more personalised. His designs generally include many references to the person whose memorial it is (Plates 6, 9 and 22).

Studio

In the early 1930s, Albert Lemmon set up a studio in rooms above a shop at 27, The Strand, Bromsgrove.[5] By the 1950s, the Strand had been designated as part of Bromsgrove High Street and the studio renumbered as 155, High Street. Lemmon maintained the studio for the rest of his life.

Access to the studio was through a ground floor shop and up stairs leading to the first floor.[6] The studio consisted of a large main room with a small room off, used to store glass, materials and equipment. In the late 1950s, the studio was equipped with benches, for cartooning, cutting and painting of glass and the leading and assembling of windows, on one long side of the room. On the opposite side were benches with a gas ring to heat soldering irons and prepare gesso. The only window in the room faced southeast. In front of this large window was a sheet of plate glass on which windows were assembled before leading. Lead lines were painted on the back of the plate glass and the pieces of painted glass held on with beeswax. A coke stove located near to the centre of the room provided heating for the studio.

It is fortunate that many of Lemmon's watercolour designs and cartoons have survived. Cartoons and a small number of designs are at the Hardman Stained Glass Studios, as already mentioned in my introduction. This 'Lemmon Archive' was given to Hardmans when Peter closed the Lemmon studio on Albert's death.

When asked to submit a design for a commission Albert Lemmon would produce a watercolour design often on a scale of one inch to one foot (Plates 8 and 17). If the donor of the window, and the church authorities approved the design, it would be sent to the Diocesan Advisory Committee. If it approved the design, the Diocesan Advisory Committee would issue a faculty for the window to be made. Once the faculty (or licence) was issue Lemmon could proceed with making the window or other art work.

At this stage, a full size cartoon would be drawn from the approved design. A window cartoon is exactly the same size and shape as the window opening and has lead lines and other details marked on it (Plates 6, 18 and 24). The cartoon is used to cut the pieces of coloured glass ready for painting details, such as faces, costume etc., according to the design. The pieces of glass are fired so that the painted detail becomes part of the glass.

The Lemmon studio did not have a kiln for firing the painted glass. Painted glass was transported in trays to Birmingham where it was fired in the kilns of Chew and Commander.[7]

The next stage was for the painted, fired glass to be assembled in leads and these cemented to make the window waterproof, before the window was erected in the window opening.

The studio used antique glass, which was mouth blown, the type favoured by Arts and Crafts stained glass makers. Peter Lemmon recalled that his father used glass made by Chance of Smethwick as well some from Powell of London in the early years of the studio. In later years, he recalled, Hartley Wood glass was used. The same representative of Hartley Wood & Co. Portobello Glass Works at Sunderland who called at the Davies studio at the Bromsgrove Guild, Gilbert Henry Wood, would also call at the Lemmon studio.[8] It is this English antique glass, with its variations of colour and thickness, which gives Lemmon's windows their bright, sparkling quality. Another feature of the windows is the narrow borders, often of white glass, which surround the figures and scenes.

His son Peter (1920-2004) assisted Lemmon in his studio. Peter Lemmon's name and initials appear alongside his father's on many of the windows and other art works. The amount of time that Peter spent in the studio is not known. I believe that he probably worked part-time with his father, as he is known to have had other employment. This included working for a glass company in Wolverhampton, where he lived during the week, returning home at weekends.

At times Albert Lemmon employed an assistant. The windows of 1927 and 1932 in All Saints Church, and the Blessed Martyrs Shrine, in St Peter's Church of 1936, in Bromsgrove, are signed DCT alongside Albert's signature (Plate 6). I suspect that Miss D C Turner, who Lemmon had met at the Bromsgrove Guild, assisted with specific commissions rather than being employed on a permanent basis.

An assistant who was employed on a permanent basis was Alan Meredith. Alan was a student of Lemmon at Bromsgrove School of Art and was later employed in his studio from 1948 to 1950 when he was conscripted to undertake National Service with the Royal Air Force. Alan Meredith recalls working with Albert Lemmon and travelling to sites to erect windows and deliver other art works, including fitting the window at Wrangle, Lincolnshire (Plate 19). Alan Meredith took up other employment after completing his National Service as Albert Lemmon was on the point of retiring.

Lemmon had occasional help with the leading, soldering and fitting of his windows as and when the need arose. He engaged Henry John Hodgetts (1879-1964) whose main employment was with A J Davies at the Bromsgrove Guild stained glass studio.[9] Another leader and fitter sometimes employed by Lemmon was a Mr Machelli.[10]

Art Teacher

Albert Lemmon was appointed Art Teacher at Bromsgrove School of Art in July 1929, a post he held until the early 1950s. The origins of the institution go back to 1860 when a new building, housing the Schools of Science and Art, opened with much ceremony in 1895, in New Road Bromsgrove.[11] It later became an Art and Technical School. In the 1930-31 sessions, Lemmon taught classes in Art and Drawing and Painting on Monday evenings, and Drawing and Painting on Wednesday and Friday evenings. In the 1940s Lemmon was still teaching Drawing and Painting each Monday, Wednesday and Friday evening. In October 1946, the Governors' Minutes record that 'the Art Group is doing good work and is well attended'.[12] This work must have provided a useful stable income for Albert Lemmon and his family.

World War II

On 11 June 1940, Albert Lemmon enrolled in the Local Defence Volunteers, serving with the 2nd Worcestershire (Bromsgrove) Battalion Home Guard throughout the war. He was discharged as Corporal Lemmon on the disbandment of the Home Guard on 31 December 1945. Peter Lemmon joined the Royal Air Force in 1940, spending much of his service in Italy.

Worcestershire Guild of Designer Craftsmen

On 23 April 1952 the inaugural meeting of the Worcestershire Guild of Artist Craftsmen, (later changed to Designer Craftsmen), was held in Bromsgrove Library. Membership of the Guild was open to 'those craftsmen whose work is considered by the Committee to have reached a very high standard and who make the greater part of their living by making and selling their work'.[13] Albert Lemmon was one of the nine founder members.[14] Later that same year the Guild held its first exhibition at Bromsgrove Art and Technical School. Lemmon exhibited a stained glass panel depicting St Christopher.

In 1953, the Guild held their second exhibition at the Birmingham and Midland Institute, Birmingham, when Lemmon exhibited eleven items. These included a 'cartoon for stained glass, the design for a Birmingham window, stained glass panels, a jewel box with 'limoges' panels, enamelled coats of arms and a gesso panel of St Margaret'. The following year the exhibition was again at the Birmingham and Midland Institute. The exhibit by Albert and Peter Lemmon 'showed the work, materials, tools and methods of the Stained Glass Artist'.[15] At the 1955 Exhibition, held at The Royal Birmingham Society of Artists Gallery, New Street, Birmingham, Lemmon's exhibits (he was now sixty-six years of age) were leaded glass shades and lanterns. At this exhibition, fourteen photographs of Guild craftsmen were also displayed. The photograph of Albert Lemmon showed him in the act of painting glass for the window he sent to Taradale, New Zealand, in memory of his brother. (Frontispiece).

The Worcestershire Guild of Designer Craftsmen flourishes today, still promoting the unique work of its members through exhibitions, teaching and demonstrations.

Signatures

The majority of the windows from the Lemmon studio are signed, as are many of the painted panels. In most windows, the name or names, are written as well as initials enclosed in a shield. Signatures are invariably to be found along the base of a window.

Lemmon's windows of 1927 and 1930 at All Saints Church and the painted panel in St Peter's Church are signed AEL and DCT (Miss D C Turner), as already mentioned. Other windows to 1938 are signed only by Albert Lemmon,

The first window to bear the additional signature of Albert's son Peter is the 1939 *Disciples at the Empty Tomb* window at St Peter's Church, West Bromwich. Peter was 19 years of age. Both Albert's and Peter Lemmon's signatures are to be found on subsequent windows. I believe that Peter's contribution was very much as an assistant to his father and in many instances his contribution was minimal. In his correspondence with me Peter always played down his role in the making of windows and other art works, perhaps this was false modesty on his part. Peter attended classes at the Birmingham School of Art like his father before him, but 'part-time for two years chiefly for life classes'.[16] The last few windows produced by the Lemmon studio from 1956 onwards, bear the signature of Peter Lemmon alone. These are at St John's Church, Bromsgrove (Plate 23), Christ Church, Catshill, Bromsgrove (Plate 25), and St Mary's Church, Sedgley. I suspect that Albert was largely responsible for these windows. There are no known windows or other art works by Peter after the death of his father.[17]

The final window, designed for St Godwold's Church, Bromsgrove, was not completed when Albert Lemmon died on 4 February 1963. It depicts St Gregory and St Anne. Peter completed the window with help of another Bromsgrove stained glass worker, Arthur Clarke, who had worked with Albert at the Bromsgrove Guild. Clarke later worked at the John Hardman Studios.[18] This final window bears the signatures of both Albert and Peter Lemmon.

1. On his letter heading, Lemmon described himself as 'Artist and Craftsman' and 'Specialist in Ecclesiastical and Historical Art' offering 'Stained Glass and the Kindred Arts, Illuminated Addresses, Decorative Painting and Mural Decoration'.
2. Letter to the author from Peter Lemmon, 15 May 2001.
3. 'The Parish Verge of All Saints' Bromsgrove', type-written manuscript by Albert Lemmon c. 1931, unsigned and undated, Worcester Records Office.
4. Robert Pancheri, who trained at the Birmingham School of Art, was one of the nine founder members, with Albert Lemmon, of the Worcestershire Guild of Designer Craftsmen.
5. The premises were used as a public house called *The Pheasant* from the 1850s until the First World War when it became a shop. Townshend, p. 17.
6. Alan Meredith recalls walking through Mrs Phillips Green Grocers shop to reach the stairs leading up to the studio. I am grateful to Alan for providing details of the studio in the late 1940s.
7. Joseph Chew established the firm of Glass and China Decorators in Bishop Street, Birmingham in 1883, which became Chew and Commander in 1901. The firm was active until 1968. Chew and Commander also fired the painted glass of Nora Yoxall and Elsie Whitford, stained glass artists, (active 1920s to 1970s) who also trained at the Birmingham School of Art (Birmingham Museum and Art Gallery, 1983).
8. Peter, in a letter dated 14 October 2002, recalled that Wood arranged to 'call early on a certain day but finally arrived late afternoon, having stayed at the Golden Cross the night the Landlord Taylor was shot by an intruder. He and the other guests had been detained by police all day'. See also Albutt, 2005, p. 15.
9. 'Harry' Hodgetts moved to Bromsgrove from Birmingham to join Davies soon after he set up the Guild studio in 1906. He also did occasional leading work for Alfred Pike in the studios of Lord Plymouth at nearby Hewell Grange, Tardebigge, Redditch.
10. Letter from Peter Lemmon to the author dated 19 December 2002.
11. Bromsgrove, Droitwich and Redditch Messenger, 28 September 1895, p. 2.
12. Minutes of Bromsgrove Higher Education Committee, Bromsgrove Art and Technical School, October 1946, p. 171.
13. Worcestershire Guild of Artist-Craftsmen, Catalogue of the Second Summer Exhibition at The Midland Institute, Birmingham, 31st August to 5th September, 1953, p. 17.
14. The founder members were Anthony Barham (furniture maker), Alice Barnwell (artist and glass engraver), Howard Bissell (potter), John Frith (furniture maker), Alan Knight (blacksmith), Leslie Ladell (furniture maker), Albert Lemmon (stained glass maker), Robert Pancheri (woodcarver and sculptor) and William Fowkes (woodworker).
15. Worcestershire Guild of Artist-Craftsmen Catalogues of Exhibitions at the Birmingham and Midland Institute, August, 1953, p. 12 and September, 1954, p. 9, and Royal Birmingham Society of Artists Galleries, Birmingham, December 1955, p. 9.
16. Peter Lemmon in a letter to the author in August 2002.
17. In 2002 I sent Peter a copy of *Angels and Oranges Stained Glass Windows in the Churches of North Kesteven,* which includes two of the Lincolnshire churches, Helpringham and Anwick, with works from the Lemmon studio. Peter replied, in a letter dated August 2002, that 'most of the windows mentioned in the book were produced by my father alone as I volunteered for the RAF in June 1940'. The windows at Helpringham, including those of 1940 and 1945 bear the signatures of both Albert and Peter. In another letter, dated 18 June 2001, Peter wrote, concerning the later windows, 'my name was used so that he could draw his old age pension'!
18. Arthur Slade Clarke, a Bromsgrove stained glass worker and newspaper cartoonist, served an apprenticeship in the A J Davis stained glass studio at the Bromsgrove Guild and later worked at the John Hardman Studios. See Kings, B, 1993.

5. Commissions

I shall discuss Lemmon's commissions by geographical location, rather than chronologically, beginning with his works in his adopted town of Bromsgrove, then Worcestershire, before going further afield.[1]

Bromsgrove
All Saints' Church

Albert Lemmon lived in the parish of All Saints and was a regular worshipper there. Both Albert and his wife Hilda served on the Parochial Church Council. Albert was also a Server and a Sidesman at the Church.

This church possesses many examples of the art works of Lemmon including his first stained glass window after setting up on his own. The two-light window, dedicated on 24 April 1927, with the faculty for Lemmon's design approved by the Diocesan Advisory Committee in November the previous year (Cover, plates 5 and 6). This window could have been the reason why Lemmon left the Guild and set up on his own. Perhaps Davies discovered that Lemmon had submitted a design on his own behalf for the window at All Saints, a commission Davies might well have expected to have been awarded to his studio.

The main lights depict the *Annunciation and St George*, with predella scenes of St Cecilia and St David representing Doris Mabel and Aneurin Weber Evans whose memorial it is. Lemmon gave a detailed account of the window, explaining the symbolism of all he included in the design. The Virgin, he wrote 'stands in meek humility receiving the wondrous news'. She is 'surrounded by Madonna lilies (purity), Marigolds (the flower of the Annunciation), Lady Smock and other flowers dedicated to her'. Detailed written explanations of his designs are a feature of the work of Lemmon. St George is portrayed 'as the historical figure of the young Roman soldier who suffered martyrdom under the Emperor Diocletian'.[2]

In the left predella St Cecilia is seated playing an organ with two children nearby, while in the right St David is shown, seated, instructing three boys. Aneurin Evans died in Flanders in 1917 while serving in the First World War. His army badge (the Worcestershire Yeomanry), a helmet and poppies of 'Flanders Fields', together with his college badge and daffodils are reminders of his life. Mabel Evans, who worshipped at All Saints' Church, was a teacher and musician who would have been acquainted with Albert Lemmon.

Lemmon used local youngsters as models for the children in the predella scenes including his own son Peter who is the smallest child at the feet of St David.[3]

As well as stained glass windows, Albert Lemmon has left examples of his considerable ability as a decorative artist in All Saints' Church. In 1931, he decorated and presented to his church a pair of churchwardens' staves and a verge (or mace) from himself and his wife Hilda (Plate 7). These beautiful objects are richly painted and gilded in gold and silver leaf, over a bas relief of gesso. They show not only Albert Lemmon's skills as a decorative artist but also his deep knowledge of the heraldry and history of the Church from early times to the present day.

The staves of the Vicar's and Parish Wardens are embellished with the heraldic arms of the parish, diocese and the royal arms and have the names of contemporary local and national figures paired with predecessors from the first millennium together with dates of appointment to their positions. The Vicar of All Saints Church, 'Edward Lumley 1929', is associated with 'S. Theodor of AD 675', on the Vicar's Wardens stave. While on the Parish Warden's Stave, the Bishop of Worcester 'Arthur Worcester Father in God 1931' is linked with 'K. Ethelred AD 675' and 'George the Fifth D V Rex Defender of the Faith' with 'K. Alfred AD 900'.

As part of a scheme extending the vestry facilities and reordering of the Lady Chapel in 1933, Albert Lemmon painted a reredos depicting the Holy Family. He has again used gesso, in this case to raise the haloes of the figures. The haloes are further accentuated with gold leaf. The sky is also of gold leaf in a manner similar to a Renaissance altarpiece. The head of Joseph may perhaps be a portrait of Lemmon's father who was a carpenter by trade.

There is also an altar with painted riddel posts, which once supported carved praying angel candlesticks, again painted by Lemmon. The angel candlesticks are presently located separately in another part of the church.

The Patronal banner of the church is also the work of Lemmon. This signed work, of paint on fabric, depicts Christ as an infant, wearing a white gown, with birds and butterflies, and flowers at his feet, including lilies, snowdrops, lily of the valley and tulips. Flowers often appear elsewhere in Lemmon's work including his stained glass windows.

Another painted banner in the church owes much to the influence of Albert Lemmon. This banner is the work of Bernard Roberson who donated it in memory of his brother Frederick Roberson who served in the Royal Engineers and was lost at Dunkirk in May 1940. It was donated to the Guild of the Servants of the Sanctuary, the Bromsgrove Chapter of St Kenelm, of which both brothers were members. Bernard was a pupil of Albert Lemmon at the School of Art in Bromsgrove and, from the style, Lemmon's influence on the design and execution of the banner is obvious.

Finstall, Bromsgrove
St Godwald's Church

Albert Lemmon painted a Patronal banner for the church of St Godwald in 1927. The fabric banner, which is 4 feet 8 inches (142 cm.) tall and 2 feet 6 inches (77 cm.) wide, depicts St Godwald as a bishop in Eucharistic vestments.[4]

Near to the base of the banner, Lemmon has painted two local scenes with relevance to the Church, which is located near to the Birmingham to Worcester railway line. One depicts the Bromsgrove carriage and wagon works, the other a steam train descending the famous Lickey Incline, a section of the Birmingham to Worcester line opened in 1840. The banner has lost much of its original colour but the art work of Albert Lemmon in the design and execution of the banner can still be appreciated.

Ten years later Albert Lemmon erected the first of two windows at St Godwald's church. This first window is in memory of Barbara Ethel Palmer, 21 years of age and Lemmon's niece. The subject of the two centre lights of this four light window is *The Annunciation*. Unusually Gabriel appears to the Virgin while she is visiting a well to draw water, according to a Celtic legend. St Barbara and St Cecilia depicted in the sidelights, together with reminders of the life of Barbara Palmer, including the badge of the local secondary school she attended, a likeness of Barbara wearing a lilac costume she wore for a musical performance of a church group, and the chalice and font of St Godwald's church.

The second window depicts St Gregory and St Anne. Albert Lemmon designed this window in 1963, the year in which he died. After Albert's death Peter Lemmon completed the window.

Bromsgrove
St Peter's Roman Catholic Church

Lemmon has a number of works in this church, which also has a family connection. Albert Lemmon's youngest sister, Anne, married Frederick Frost (1872-1947) a Roman Catholic, and converted to his faith. Both Anne and Frederick worshipped at St Peter's and are buried in the churchyard. Anne, who was ten years younger than Albert, died in 1956.

A panel painting by Lemmon dedicated on Sunday 22 March 1936, depicts the English saints John Fisher and Thomas More. It is a triptych, which he painted using tempera colours and gold leaf on a gessoed wooden panel. The figures of St John Fisher and St Thomas More are depicted standing wearing ecclesiastical vestments each holding the palm of martyrdom. Between them stands the figure of Christ the King.

The men were martyred in 1535 for failing to take the oath making Henry VIII supreme head of the Church of England. Fisher and More were beatified in 1886 and canonised in May 1935. The English Martyrs Shrine, as it is known, dedicated only ten months after the canonisation must be among the earliest memorials to the saints.

Below the main panels is a Latin inscription naming the donors of the shrine. The donors were the artist, Albert Lemmon, and his sister Anne Frost, who donated the panel in memory of their sisters. The other donor was William Moore.

Two smaller panels painted by Lemmon, displayed near to the Martyrs' Shrine, depict the Blessed John Wall and St Teresa.

Lemmon was commissioned to make a stained glass window donated by Miss Harriet Hanson as a memorial to the Hanson family. To commission a window in 1941 or 1942 was a great act of faith considering the uncertainty of the times. Enemy aircraft passed over the area on their way to bomb the industrial West Midlands. This three light window, dedicated on Sunday 28th June 1942, is perhaps the most outstanding of Lemmon's smaller windows.[5] Lemmon has depicted St Peter, the fisherman, standing in a sailing ship, the 'Barca Petri', holding the keys to heaven. He also holds the ends of a net having caught various fishes and a crab. At the top of the mast, in the main tracery light, stands a cockerel, a reminder of Peter's denial of Christ before the crucifixion. This powerful image, with St Peter in the centre light, standing in a brown boat with water and sky in a rich blue enclosing the scene, has less of the intricate personal details relating to the donors, which Lemmon introduced into many of his designs.

Other Bromsgrove Windows

There are two more windows by Lemmon in the Bromsgrove area. A *St Cecilia* window, in memory of schoolmaster and organist, is at Bromsgrove Methodist Church. This window of about 1957, was relocated to the newly built Methodist Church in 1983.

In what is now Housman House, of Bromsgrove School, is a two-light window depicting scenes of Bromsgrove in 1634. When the windows were commissioned, the building was the Perry Hall Hotel.[6] There are two lights of two panels each. The scenes represent Bromsgrove in 1634. Depicted is the town crier, a maid serving drinks, a man in stocks as well as Perry Hall and St John's Church, Bromsgrove.

Three Worcestershire Churches
Evesham, Bengeworth
St Peter's Church
There are thee stained glass windows of 1937, 1938 and 1954 at Bengeworth. The earliest depicts *Christ in his Father's Workshop*. This is a theme much explored by Lemmon in stained glass and panel paintings. The window shows Christ as a young man sawing a plank of wood. Around Christ, on bench and floor, lie the carpenters tools with which Lemmon would have been familiar as a youth through his father's occupation.

The window of 1954 depicts the *Vision of Eoves*, the sixth century swineherd who saw a vision of the Virgin (Plate 22). Eoves, who kneels before the vision, wears a blue garment beneath a red cloak. He has a pig at his side. It was on this spot that the town of Evesham grew up around the Abbey founded to commemorate the vision. Also depicted in the window are St Peter's Church, the Bell Tower of the former Abbey and fruit and vegetables – strawberries, plums, potatoes, cabbage and parsnips – produced in the fertile earth of the Vale of Evesham. The window, dedicated to Frances Albert Wells, whose image appears in the single tracery light, standing at his woodworker's bench making the rood screen which still adorns the chancel arch of St Peter's Church.

Rowney Green, Alvechurch
Shared Church (Methodist)
Probably Lemmon's only circular window is to be found in the now Shared Church, former Methodist, in the village of Rowney Green near Alvechurch. The window depicts a seated Christ with two children.

Little Witley
St Michael and All Angels Church
The Friends of Saint Michael's Church donated this two-light window in the west wall of the church, in 1953. The left light depicts St Michael wearing armour with ruby wings stretching high into the light. Below St Michael is a predella scene of the outside of the church from the north-east. In the right light another angel, with matching wings wearing a white gown has his hand on the head of a child. In this predella is the church font with a river flowing behind it. This river might the local Shrawley Brook, the nearby River Severn or perhaps the River Jordan? The Church still has Lemmon's water-colour design which is signed 'A E Lemmon Artist and Craftsman Bromsgrove'. A letter of the time asks for donations towards the £150 the window cost.

Birmingham and the Black Country

Churches in the conurbation of Birmingham and the Black Country to the north of Bromsgrove provided Lemmon with a large number of commissions.

Birmingham, Ladywood
St Margaret's Church

It is highly likely that the Lemmon family worshipped at this church, which was located at the junction of Ledsam Street and Alston Street, only a few yards from 17, Alston Street, where the Lemmon family lived.

On 8 November 1911, a faculty granted to St Margaret's Church, Ladywood 'to erect and place a stained glass window in the Baptistery wall'. The Vestry Minutes dated 12 October 1911, which agreed to the submission of a faculty, notes that the window will be 'in accordance with the design submitted by Mr Lemmon'.[7] Could this be the very first window that the recently trained Albert Lemmon was solely responsible for designing? The design by Lemmon, a coloured copy of which is with the faculty documents, was for a lancet window depicting *Christ Blessing Children*. The bearded figure of Christ is shown wearing a traditional white robe with a blue cloak around his shoulders but the three children in the design wear modern clothing. The window was in memory of a former priest, Father Arthur Orlando Cherrington, who had been Vicar of St Margaret's for 21 years. It is not known whether Lemmon's design was actually made by him or one of the local stained glass firms. St Margaret's Church, deemed redundant, was demolished in 1956. This window, the earliest known design by Lemmon, may have been lost with the demolition, sold or relocated to another church in the Birmingham Diocese.

Birmingham, Aston
Church of God, former All Souls Church

There are two windows by the Lemmon studio in the former All Souls Church. The east window, called the *All Souls* or *Spirit of Birmingham* window, is based on revelations 21 vv 1-7, which begins 'And I saw a new heaven and a new earth'. This large, five-light window has nineteen tracery lights. Lemmon himself undoubtedly wrote the leaflet, giving a description of the window, presumably printed for its consecration.[8] He tells us that the iconography of the window is divided into three parts; 'the upper portion representing the Godhead and His powers, the centre portion the Redeemer and His Saints of all ages and the lower part symbolises the spirit of Birmingham'.

In the tracery lights are seven cherubim and the Archangels Gabriel and Michael around the 'Flame of the Eternal Father'. The central section has Christ upon a rainbow with saints. As well as traditional saints, such as the Virgin, St Anne, St Agnes, St John and St Peter, Lemmon has included living or recently dead persons, both ecclesiastic and lay people. Interestingly some traditional saints have the face of a local twentieth individual. St Philip has the face of Dr Russell Wakefield a former Bishop of Birmingham, St Chad resembles Dr Oldknow once vicar of nearby Bordesley, while Dr Charles Gore, the first Bishop of Birmingham, who consecrated All Souls Church in 1907 is depicted as himself. Miss Kathleen Unite, a benefactor of the church who laid the foundation stone, is also among the saints. Pre-eminent figures in the 'Spirit of Birmingham', along the lower edge of the window, are bearers from the city arms, a man and a woman, who are kneeling in the outermost lights. The woman represents art and has a book and an artists' palette nearby. The man, dressed as a smith, has an anvil and hammer near him. Other figures include a girl wearing her confirmation veil and a priest baptising a child. There are many city buildings in this section, including the University, Art Gallery, St Philip's Cathedral, even All Souls Vicarage. In the central light, the Tree of Life grows in Birmingham's Victoria Square.

The details I have given here are only a part of the complex iconography devised by Albert Lemmon for this *Spirit of Birmingham* window. It must have taken a considerable time to devise the scheme and paint the watercolour design for the approval of the church and diocesan authorities. The unveiling of the window to commemorate the 25th anniversary of the consecration of the church must have been a grand affair.

All Souls Church became redundant as an Anglican Church in 1981. The Church of God (Universal) now worships there.

Birmingham, Balsall Heath
St Paul's Church

When the congregation of St Paul's Church in Balsall Heath moved to a new building in 1980, they took with them stained glass panels from windows in the old building. These panels, one is by Lemmon, two more by the firm of T W Camm of Smethwick, hang in the chancel.[9] The Lemmon panel depicts a standing St Paul and is a thank offering for Alice Williams and her daughter who were involved in an accident.

The St Paul window was probably erected in the 1930s. The Reverend Gordon Robertson was assistant vicar from 1934 to 1937, when he moved to St Andrew's Church, Helpringham in Lincolnshire. Having seen the stained glass by Albert Lemmon at Balsall Heath, The Reverend Robertson later employed him at Helpringham.

West Bromwich, Greets Green
St Peter's Church
The Church of St Peter at Greets Green, West Bromwich, has three windows by Lemmon. The four-light east window was known to me through the water-colour design in the Lemmon display at Bromsgrove Museum. It was not until I was recording Lemmon cartoons at the John Hardman Studios that I became aware of its location at Greets Green (Plate 9). The faculty was approved on 6 March 1930 and the window donated by parishioners.

This is a stunning *Te Deum* window, creating a wall of colour above the altar. Heaven is depicted in the tracery and the four Archangels in the heads of the lights. Below them, Christ in a white gown stands in a blue and purple mandorla of birds in flight. At the same level are depicted the Virgin and many crowned saints including St Peter and St John the Baptist. Also included is the then vicar of St Peter's, The Reverend Lamplugh, who was 'very well thought of' and whose inclusion was at the insistence of parishioners. Kneeling, lower in the scene, are a man, a woman and a girl and boy representing the parishioners. The man wears a striped shirt with the sleeves rolled up representing the Black Country workers of the parish. The girl holds a doll and flowers, while the boy, dressed in a blue Cubs uniform, has a pigeon perched on his hand and his dog by his side. I wonder whether these were actual members of the congregation. Rabbits, a tortoise and a lamb are also there to praise God in this *Te Deum* window. A narrow predella scene of the Last Supper stretches across the base of the four lights of the window separated from the scene above by a grapevine. This large window is full of colour and interest and contains over forty angel and human faces.

Halesowen, West Midlands
St Margaret's Church
In the five-light east window at St Margaret's Church, Hasbury, Halesowen, Lemmon has depicted Christ with the Virgin and St John the Baptist in the centre lights with St Margaret and St Kenelm in the outer lights (Plate 10). The church is dedicated to St Margaret and St Kenelm is a local saint. St Kenelm, the son of a King of Mercia, was supposedly murdered at the instigation of his sister at nearby Clent. Lemmon has depicted this little known saint holding the axe with which he was murdered. Next to him is the white bull, which (according to one legend) guided searchers to his body. These five standing figures make an impressive east window. They are set in a largely white background in order to allow light into church.

Sedgley, Dudley
St Mary's Church
St Mary's Church has a series of single light memorial windows, four by Albert Lemmon, from 1942 to 1952, and a fifth signed by Peter Lemmon alone of 1962 the year before Albert's death.

Both Albert and Peter Lemmon signed the windows made in 1948 and 1952. I believe that Peter was very much the assistant to Albert at this time. The 1962 window has documentary evidence in the form of a letter on Peter's headed notepaper dated March 1962. These windows, with their bold colours and compact designs make a pleasing addition among the many other stained glass windows in the church. All five Lemmon windows are in the south wall of the nave of St Mary's Church.

The earliest window depicts *St Francis Preaching to the Birds* with two children, with their dog, apparently also listening. In the background are a school and church as the window is in memory of David Hughes Hartland who served for 30 years at St Mary's School. The adjacent window, depicting *St Elizabeth and St John the Baptist* is also in memory of David Hartland. Archive material tells that this window was to be a memorial to Mrs Hartland but in order to secure the window opening next to her husband's St Francis window she had the window fitted as an additional memorial to her husband. *St Christopher*, a window of 1949, in memory of Arthur Howes, who was 'Chorister, Crucifer and Server in this Church for 50 Years' (Plate 20). The inscription is at the base of the window held by children who kneel in front of the font and processional cross of the church. I wonder whether these children could be grand-children of this long-serving member of the church.

The third window, in memory of Joseph and Harriet Nichols, has the *Holy Family* as its subject. The faces of Joseph and Mary are familiar from other windows and paintings of the same subject.

Lye, Stourbridge
Christ Church
Albert Lemmon's commission was for three figurative stained glass windows, and two using plain cathedral glass in rectangular quarries with a minimum use of colour in the borders.

In 1951 stained glass windows were erected in the east walls of the south and north transepts. The south transept window is a memorial to the dead of the Second World War. Lemmon devised a scheme to create a war memorial chapel in the transept which, in addition to the stained glass, would have included an oak altar, a painted cross and candlesticks, cornice and riddel posts and curtains. This scheme was abandoned during what was a period of austerity following the war when the raising of funds for a more ambitious project might have proved to be something of a burden on the congregation.

The war memorial window depicts a standing Christ holding a chalice administering Holy Communion to kneeling uniformed service personnel representing the Army, Royal Air Force, Navy and nursing services against a red curtain (Plate 21). The predella bears the names of 49 men 'of this parish who gave their lives in the Second World War'. In the left light Lemmon has depicted the famous Flanders Poppy, surely a poignant reminder of his days in the trenches in the First World War and of his son Peter's service abroad with the RAF in the Second World War. Next to the poppies are the initials of both craftsmen in shields as well as 'A E & P E Lemmon fecit Bromsgrove 1951' along the lower edge of this light. A recent research project to contact the relatives of those named in the window to invite them to a service of remembrance held at the church to commemorate the sixtieth anniversary of the ending of the Second World War in Europe proved to be very successful.

The window in the east wall of the north transept depicts the *Good Shepherd*. It is in memory of the Reverend William Smith who was Vicar of Christ Church from 1933 to 1948. The north transept has been re-ordered, as have other parts of the church, with the result that the transept now has ground floor and first floor rooms. The re-ordering has meant that the window has been bisected by the floor of the upper room. The re-ordering of many churches has made them more able to respond to the needs of their congregations and the parishes they serve by providing improved facilities.

The third figurative window by Lemmon at Christ Church was 'The Gift of Thomas Henry Hodgkiss, Churchwarden, as a Thankoffering to God AD 1952'. In the upper section of the window, a figure of St Andrew stands holding a fishing net and a gaff in front of a saltire cross. To the left Worcester Cathedral is depicted and to the right Christ Church. The lower third of the window has Andrew and Peter in their fishing boat being called by Christ to become his disciples. The wide border to the window has the names of continents with the heads of indigenous inhabitants, including a Red Indian with a feathered headdress for America, a black man for Africa and a native Australian. The inclusion of America and Australia is surely a reference to the spread of Christianity throughout the world, as well as St Andrew's supposed missionary work.

Birmingham Children's Hospital Chapel

The hospital chapel was damaged during an air raid in the Second World War and the Lemmon window destroyed. The subject of the window, befitting a hospital chapel, was the patron saints of nurses and children, *St Barnabus and St Nicholas*.

Birmingham, Erdington
Highcroft Hall Hospital Chapel
This hospital chapel, in the Erdington district of Birmingham had a painted altar front and a tester beam (and possibly other painted memorial panels at the west end of the chapel) by Lemmon. The chapel has been demolished and the site redeveloped. The present location of these items is unknown.

Birmingham, Edgbaston
St James' Church
The redundant church of St James, Edgbaston has been adapted to provide living accommodation. A document of 1970 tantalisingly mentions a reredos by Lemmon in the north transept. There is no record of what happened to the reredos before the church was sold to developers.

Birmingham, Small heath
St Gregory's Church
The former St Gregory's Church in Small Heath, Birmingham was made redundant by the Church of England and sold to the Bethel United Church as recently as 1997. Lemmon's reredos and a number of his panel paintings in the Lady Chapel on the south side were removed. I have so far been unable to locate them.

Tividale, Dudley
St Michael's Church
When St Michael's Church, Tividale relocated to a new building a place was not found for the Lemmon window of 1940 depicting *St Elizabeth and St John the Baptist*. The window was probably sold. The present location is unknown.

West Bromwich
Christ Church
Designs for windows in the now demolished Christ Church are known from Lemmon's watercolour designs and cartoons (Plate 8). The watercolours are particularly pleasing works of art in their own right. The windows were presumably sold and, it is to be hoped, now adorn another building.

Wolverhampton
St George's Church
St George's Church was not entirely demolished; part was incorporated into a new supermarket! The designs Lemmon stained glass windows are known from tracings

of designs with the faculties and from the cartoons. The windows, it is believed, were sold.

I would be delighted to learn where windows from demolished and redundant churches are now located and have included them in the gazetteer under their original location.

Lincolnshire
There are windows and other art works by Lemmon in five churches within a ten-mile radius, in southeast Lincolnshire. This Lincolnshire enclave of works by Lemmon is due to the influence of The Reverend Gordon Robertson. The Reverend Robertson was Assistant Priest at St Paul's Church, Balsall Heath when Lemmon's St Paul window was completed there in 1936. In 1938 he became Vicar of Helpringham and suggested Lemmon to Mrs Watts for the restoration of the north chapel at Helpringham, a commission that was completed in 1940.

Helpringham, Lincolnshire
St Andrew's Church
In 1939, Lemmon submitted a watercolour design to restore the north aisle chapel of St Andrew's Church 'to its ancient use'. Mrs S K Watts funded the work in memory of her husband Robert Knowles Watts. Lemmon's original design is still in the possession of the family. This is probably his first work involving the combining of stained glass work with other decorative arts as an entity.

The scheme consists of a stained glass window in the east wall of the chapel, above a stone altar, which carries a reredos, also the work of Lemmon, in the form of a triptych. Completing the scheme are a pair of painted wooden candlesticks, a painted wooden cut-out image of St Hugh of Avalon and a painted pelican in her piety on the aumbry door.

This three-light stained glass window has Christ in Majesty in the centre light (Plate 12). Lemmon has made much use red and blue glass in this window and an impressive use of white glass for the light spreading across the window, emanating from Christ's halo. In the left light, St Hugh holds a model of Lincoln Cathedral and has his swan at his side. The right light shows St Andrew with a model of the church. Scenes at the base of the outer lights depict St Hugh before a king (Henry II or Richard I) and Christ calling St Andrew. Beneath the figure of Christ in the central light Lemmon has added the house and garden of Richard Watts. In the heads of the lights are three archangels, Gabriel, Michael and Raphael, and above them in the tracery lights, cherubim.

Lemmon's painted reredos shows the Resurrected Christ above the empty tomb with a seated Angel of the Resurrection with disciples in the side panels (Plate 13). Depicted on the outer panels are St Peter and St John and the two Marys arriving at the empty tomb. Lemmon has used a great deal of gold leaf as the background and border. The outer panels of this triptych close to reveal a night scene with Christ, at prayer in the Garden of Gethsemane, being handed a chalice by an angel robed in blue with blue wings. This sombre scene for Christ's passion has only the nimbuses, chalice and the border highlighted with gold leaf.

A second Lemmon window, erected in the north wall of the chapel in 1943, was donated by Edward Robinson in memory of Cecil Robinson of Quadring and Tom White of Spalding. This window is a celebration of many local Lincolnshire parishes. The main images in the window are St Luke in the centre light, holding a book and quill and with an impressive bull's head at his side, with St Gilbert and Bishop Edward of Lincoln. In the heads of the main lights and the tracery lights are depicted images and names of the nearby churches of Quadring, Spalding and Hale, as well as Lincoln Cathedral. Above the image of St Gilbert is the interior of Sempringham with members of the Gilbertine Order, which he founded, bearing his coffin. The interior of Heckington Church, depicted above Bishop Edward, includes the Easter procession before the Easter sepulchre.

The commissioning of the restoration of the chapel in 1940 and the window of 1943 were acts of great faith on the part of the donors considering that this was during the Second World War when Lincolnshire, together with much of southern and eastern England, was especially vulnerable to aerial attack from mainland Europe. At this time also Lemmon's son Peter was serving as ground crew with the Royal Air Force in Italy.

Following the Second World War Lemmon received more commissions from the parishioners of St Andrew's Church. This time he produced a window for the south wall of the nave and refurbished the Lady Chapel in the south aisle, as a War Memorial. The window, of 1945, has a complex iconography. The main figures depicted are the Virgin and Child, St Paul and St Peter, but the Seven Sacraments form the dominant theme with the names of the fallen, inscribed near to the base of the window, to represent the sacrament of burial. By 1947 Lemmon completed the Memorial Chapel with the addition painted wooden items including an altar cross and two painted wooden candlesticks, four additional candlesticks – two free standing and two mounted on corbels, and an altar rail. On the south wall of the same chapel Lemmon provided a painted panel depicting a Pieta as well as a wall mounted, wooden, memorial tablet bearing the names of war dead. Many of the individual items were donated by members of the congregation in memory of those mentioned on the memorial tablet.

Quadring, Lincolnshire
St Margaret's Church

In 1945 Lemmon was commissioned to restore the north aisle chapel, in a manner similar to his work at Helpringham. The commission was in memory of Edward Robinson and was donated by his brothers and sisters. The work consists of a stained glass window above a painted altar front with a matching painted wooden altar cross and candlesticks, a painted aumbry door and three painted cut-outs depicting St Bernard, St Margaret and St Cecelia.

The window has Christ in majesty in the centre light (Plate 16). He stands in front of a rainbow and has a glowing red halo with pink and yellow rays of light emanating from Him across all three lights. A ploughman and sower are present in the left light, and a young girl and a Bishop of Lincoln (surely a portrait) in the right. The plough is of the horse-drawn type. There is an interesting local association at the base of the lights including the home of the Robinson family, as well as examples of the agricultural and horticultural products for which the region is famous, including wheat, potatoes, root vegetables, tulips and crocuses. In the tracery lights angels representing night and day, winter and summer, and the seasons look down upon the scene.

Lemmon has embellished the three-panelled oak altar with a painted *Annunciation*. Mary and Gabriel kneel facing one another separated by a dove enclosed within a circular rainbow emanating gold tongues. The figures are wearing blue and white gowns and blue is the dominant colour of the Lemmon cross and candlesticks on the altar. The cross bears an image of Adam with his arms outstretched, a link with the window above which has Adam and Eve kneeling beneath the Tree of Knowledge with the serpent between them.

Anwick, Lincolnshire
St Edith's Church

Lemmon designed and made a Second World War memorial window for St Edith's Church in 1947. The main figures are a seated St Mary (Our Lady of Lincoln) with the Christ Child, a standing St Edith and St George. Beneath these figures are scenes relating to local agriculture and to wartime. Below Edith is a wheat harvest with a figure of a nurse. In the right light a soldier looks out to sea where battleships lie offshore and landing craft approach the shore. In the central light a boy and girl place a poppy wreath in a grave with St Edith's Church in the background.

The window is 'Offered to God in Thanksgiving for Peace and in Honour of all Men and Women who served in the War 1939-1945', and in memory of two named war dead of the parish, Charles Geoffrey Newton and Reginald Holland.

A window of 1952 by Lemmon commemorates the 800th Anniversary of the church (1150-1950). The window is in the children's corner and depicts a young Christ surrounded by scenes that include many plants and animals. Christ stands in a summer landscape with winter and autumn scenes in the outer lights.

Metheringham, Lincolnshire
St Wilfrid's Church

This three-light window has three main figures, St Mary and the Christ Child in the centre flanked by St Elizabeth, with distaff and spinning wheel, and St Joseph leaning on his carpenters' bench.

In the tracery lights is a church tower with bells. Lemmon's original design is annotated and tells us that these are the 'Bells of Crowland'.[10] This upper part of the window is a celebration of the influence of the monastic orders in Lincolnshire. The bell-tower masonry has carved statues of St Guthlac, St Gilbert and St Hugh. In the heads of the main lights Lemmon has depicted Sisters of the Gilbertine Order, Cistercian Monks and, in the central light, three Benedictine Monks of Crowland pull on ropes to ring the bells in the tracery above their heads.

Wrangle, Lincolnshire
St Mary and St Nicholas Church

It was in 1949 that the church at Wrangle received a four-light window by Lemmon (Plates 17, 18 and 19). The theme of the window is *The Incarnation*. Lemmon wrote that he was 'following the old medieval custom of recording past incidents in a setting of our own particular period, Our Lord and His Mother are supported by historical and present day figures'.[11]

The historical figures are St Hugh of Lincoln and St Nicholas, the patron of the church, in the outer lights are dressed in richly coloured vestments. The central lights have six figures representing present day 'manhood and womanhood' grouped around a seated St Mary and the Christ Child. The figures represent people of various ages, from a seated lad holding a goldfish in a bowl to an elderly couple. The elderly couple are particularly engaging – the woman wears spectacles and is knitting. Lemmon's models were surely parishioners of Wrangle!

In the tracery-lights are a sun, moon, a corona of angels representing the seasons, and the sun and the rain. Each of the angels of the seasons has an appropriate plant; summer has honeysuckle, autumn a hazelnut branch, winter holly with its berries and spring narcissi.

New Zealand
Taradale
All Saints Church[12]

There are windows from the Lemmon studio in All Saints Church, Taradale, which is near Napier on the east coast of North Island, New Zealand.

A window dedicated in 1956 is in memory of George Frank Lemmon, Albert's brother, known to Albert and Peter as Frank (Plate 24). Frank Lemmon had six sons who served abroad in the Second World War and he had intended to dedicate a window, designed and made by his brother, as a thanksgiving for their safe return. This did not happen and it was Frank's wife, Elsie Edith, who commissioned the window after the death of her husband. A report of the dedication of the window states that 'three sons of Mr G Lemmon, Messrs Eric, Raymond and Norman Lemmon – having received minute instructions from their uncle in England, took out the old east window and put in the new one – a delicate and difficult task which they carried through without a hitch in less than two days'.[13] In the upper section of this three light window are depicted Christ in Glory, the Virgin Mary and St George. A man and woman, representing craftsmanship and labour, and arts and learning, kneel at the base of the outer lights. Also in each outer light are three standing figures that make an interesting link between New Zealand and England. The left light has likenesses of the first bishop of New Zealand, Bishop Selwyn (later Bishop of Lichfield), Bishop Bennet, first Maori Bishop, and a young Maori girl. The right light has representatives of the armed services. A soldier and airman in New Zealand service uniforms stand next to Captain Cooke who represent the Navy. The window has many small details including a Maori house, a kiwi, ferns and the heraldic arms of Hawke Bay, Napier, the Diocese of Birmingham and the Diocese of Waiapu.

Lemmon's design follows a familiar format with Christ, saints and angels in the upper half above likenesses of real people together with objects related to the church below, in this case All Saints, Taradale, New Zealand. By including representatives of the armed forces, he has made passing reference to his brother's six sons who returned safely from overseas war service. Albert Lemmon wrote a 'Description of (the) East Window, All Saints, Taradale' in which he explained the significance of everything he had included in his design. This description was included in a booklet printed by the Lemmon family and donated to the church.[14]

The other windows at Taradale, dedicated in 1960, depict *St Cecilia* and *St Andrew*. Only Peter Lemmon's signature appears on these windows, unlike the first, which bears the signatures of both Albert and his son. Waldo Anderson, who was a member of the choir at All Saints Church, donated these windows. They are located above the choir stall he had occupied.

Silian, Ceredigion
St Sulian's Church
St Sulian's Church has a three-light window with St Mary, Christ and St David as the main figures, and predella scenes with St Margaret, St Columba and St Dubritus. The predella panels have typical homely depictions by Lemmon. St Margaret is knitting while watching over a little girl playing with a doll, nearby a hen cares for her chicks (Plate 11). St Columba is seated teaching three children at his feet. The lad on the right has his arm around the neck of his dog and a bird perched on the right hand.

Thornborough, Buckinghamshire
St Mary's Church
Lemmon was commissioned to design and make a stained glass window for St Mary's Church, erected in 1944, and in 1946, in the sanctuary, a Second World War Memorial.

The window design, which is similar to a window at St Peter's Church, Bengeworth, Evesham, shows Jesus as a youth at work in his father Joseph's workshop (Plate 14). The distant landscape 'shows Thornborough today' Lemmon tells us in his explanation of the window available in the church.

In the chancel, Lemmon created a memorial consisting of a reredos and altar candlesticks, sanctuary screen with rood and an honour board. The sanctuary screen is in three sections of low, unpainted oak panels separated by four upright posts. The posts support a beam with painted Navy, RAF and Army regiment badges. The beam bears a painted wooden, cut-out rood with lavish use of gold leaf (Plate 15). Crucified Christ looks down at His grieving mother, standing on the left, with St John on the right. An inscription on a sanctuary door tells us that 'The Sanctuary Screen was given by Thornborough Service Men and Women in Thanksgiving for safe return from the War'. The rood donated in memory of Flight Sergeant Cyril Frank Capel. Within the sanctuary, a Roll of Honour Board has the names of 47 service personnel, including Captain Gladys Tomkins ATS, with their rank and the unit in which they served. The reredos consists of three separate painted panels, fixed to the existing wall panelling, in memory of Christopher Martin Brown. In the central panel, Lemmon has depicted the risen Christ. In the left panel, a seated mother nurses a baby, with a boy kneeling at her side, watched over by the Mother of Christ. The right panel has a Royal Marine 'who represents all of the three services, who gave their earthly lives in the war. A youthful symbol of knighthood in the present age; the S. George of England modernised into the valiant boy of Britain' as Lemmon tells us in his description of the reredos.

Restoration Work
Bishopstone, Herefordshire
St Lawrence
Lemmon undertook two restoration commissions at St Lawrence's Church. In 1954, he reset a group of nine panels in the south chancel window. The panels, the collection of a former vicar of the parish, form an eclectic group of English and Continental stained glass, dating from the sixteenth to the nineteenth century. Lemmon set the glass 'in a clear and simple setting, made with the finest Antique glass'.

Lemmon also repainted the carved reredos and panelling at the east end of the church which dates in part from the sixteenth century. Lemmon painted kneeling figures of St Lawrence and St Mary to the central cartouches, as part of the restoration.

Unlocated Works
Two windows, which I have been unable to locate, I know of one from the cartoon, the other from photographs in the Lemmon photograph album. The cartoon depicts *St George*, his head surely a portrait, in armour and cloak, with his sword resting upon the head of the vanquished dragon.[15] The other, known from photographs of the cartoon and the window, is of two lights and depicts *Christ Blessing Children and St George*. The photographs are annotated 'Cartoon and Colour Sketch for window (Sheffield)'.

Lost or Relocated?
The locations of some of Lemmon's stained glass windows and other art works are at present unknown. The buildings for which they were commissioned, may be known, and details obtained from faculties, watercolour designs, cartoons, newspaper reports and other sources, but the building may be no longer extant due to war damage or demolition or, having been made redundant, put to another use. Today it is usual to record any dispersed artworks when a church ceases to be required for worship. Unfortunately, in the past this was not the case.

I would be pleased to learn the whereabouts of any relocated works from the Lemmon studio, especially those mentioned in the Gazetteers.

---

[1] Gazetteers at the end of this book contain details of Lemmon's work in stained glass and his other art works.

[2] All Saints Church, Order of Service, Dedication of Memorial Window, April 24, 1927.

[3] In a letter to the author, dated 29 January 2004, Peter Lemmon mentions the names of other children depicted in the window.

4   French, Sonia and Tom, 'The Patronal Banner of St Godwald', in, *St Godwald's Parish Magazine*, October 2006, pp. 16-19. Lammas, Pete, 'Banner will once again be pride of the parish', in *Bromsgrove Advertiser*, March 2007.

5   See Albutt, R, 2002, p. 37, for a photograph of this window.

6   Perry Hall Hotel was formerly the home of the Housman family, including A E Housman (1859-1936), poet and classicist, his sister Clemence (1861-1955), illustrator and novelist, and their brother Laurence (1865-1959), dramatist, illustrator and novelist. Their father Edward (1831-1894) was a Bromsgrove Solicitor. His father, The Reverend Thomas Housman (1795-1870) was the first vicar at Christ Church in the village of Catshill, two miles north of Bromsgrove. Christ Church, Catshill has a processional cross and a stained glass window by Albert and Peter Lemmon respectively. It is interesting to note that A E Housman was educated at Bromsgrove School which now uses his former home as a boarding establishment.

7   Birmingham Diocesan Records at Birmingham Central Library, reference BDR/C6/1/157.

8   *All Souls' Parish Church, Witton, A Description of the East Window. Erected to Commemorate the 25th Anniversary of the Consecration of the Church*, [n.p., n. pub., n.d.].

9   The panels by T W Camm were designed by Walter Camm and executed Florence, Robert and Walter Camm. Thomas William Camm founded the firm in 1888. Three of his children, Florence, Robert and Walter, joined the company, all of them trained at Birmingham School of Art. Florence attended classes for many years and was acquainted with Albert Lemmon. The panels at St Paul's Church are from an Annunciation window.

10   Lemmon's original design for the Metheringham window is part of the Lemmon Archive at John Hardman.

11   Undated booklet produced by the church, written by Lemmon, *Description of Memorial Window in Lady Chapel of Our Lady and St Nicholas, Wrangle*.

12   My thanks to The Revd Gerald Clarke for kindly sending me material on the windows at Taradale.

13   Herald Tribune, Monday, 2 July 1956.

14   Lemmon A E, *The Parish Church of All Saints, Taradale, Description and Explanation of Figures and Symbols Depicted in Our East Window Which Bears the Inscription 'To the Glory of God'*, (Napier: Daily Telegraph, 1957).

15   Albutt, Roy, 'A E Lemmon Stained Glass Cartoon of St George and the Dragon', in *The Bromsgrove Society Newsletter*, 24, 3, (September 2004).

6. Conclusion

Albert Lemmon was born in the slums of Ladywood in Birmingham at the end of the Victorian era and trained at the Birmingham Municipal School of Art at the beginning of the Twentieth century. He lived the rest of his life in the small market town of Bromsgrove, in north Worcestershire, with the exception of a brief period in Glasgow (1909-c. 1911) and during the Great War (1915-1919).

At Bromsgrove he met his wife Hilda and settled there where he found an outlet for his considerable artistic talents undertaking commissions in his studio and teaching at the local School of Art.

Lemmon worked first as an assistant to A J Davies in the stained glass studio at the Bromsgrove Guild gaining valuable practical experience. Then in 1927, he established his own studio where he designed and made over sixty, often stunning, stained glass windows, as well as leaded lights, and he produced a wide range of richly decorated items of an ecclesiastical nature. His work is to be found in churches mainly in the English Midlands.

Lemmon remained true to the Arts and Crafts ethos under which he trained at Birmingham School of Art. He undertook all aspects of the design and making of stained glass windows and decorative art works. His studio was mainly a one-man affair during the thirty-six years that it flourished.

The work he produced, with the detailed written explanations of the religious significance of all elements of the designs, suggests the he was a deeply religious man. Lemmon was a churchgoer, an Anglo-Catholic.

Albert Lemmon lies in an unmarked grave in Bromsgrove cemetery. The remains of his wife Hilda, and son Peter, who never married, interred with him. Lemmon's memorial is the works of art he produced for locations mentioned in this book. The makers' name and that of his son are indicated inconspicuously on the works for those who might be interested.

1. National Medal for Success in Art awarded by the Board of Education to Albert Lemmon as a student at the Birmingham School of Art. The inscription along the edge reads *Albert E Lemmon Design for Stained Glass, 1907*.

2. St Valentine's Day Card, by Albert Lemmon, sent to Hilda Bridgman in 1914. Albert and Hilda were married on 1 January 1918.

3. *Yuletide Greetings* **(1919)** cover of book of drawings by Albert Lemmon while he was on active service with the Cameron Highlanders in the First World War.

4. *Yuletide Greetings,* p. 11, *New Year 1918*.

5. Bromsgrove, All Saints, *Annunciation and St George*, 1927, (detail).

6. Bromsgrove, All Saints, *Annunciation and St George,* 1927, cartoon (detail).

7. Bromsgrove, All Saints, Church Warden's Stave, 1931.

8. West Bromwich, Christ Church (demolished), design for *St Aiden, St Augustine and St Chad*, 1928.

9. West Bromwich, Greets Green, St Peter, *Te Deum*, 1930.

10. **Halesowen,** St Margaret, *Christ with Saints*, 1935.

11. **Silian,** St Sulian, *Christ, St Mary and St David*, 1936, (detail).

12. Helpringham, St Andrew, *Christ, St Hugh and St Andrew*, 1940.

13. Helpringham, St Andrew, Reredos, *Resurrection*, 1940.

14. Thornborough, St Mary, *Christ in Joseph's Workshop*, 1944.

15. Thornborough, St Mary, Rood Screen, 1946.

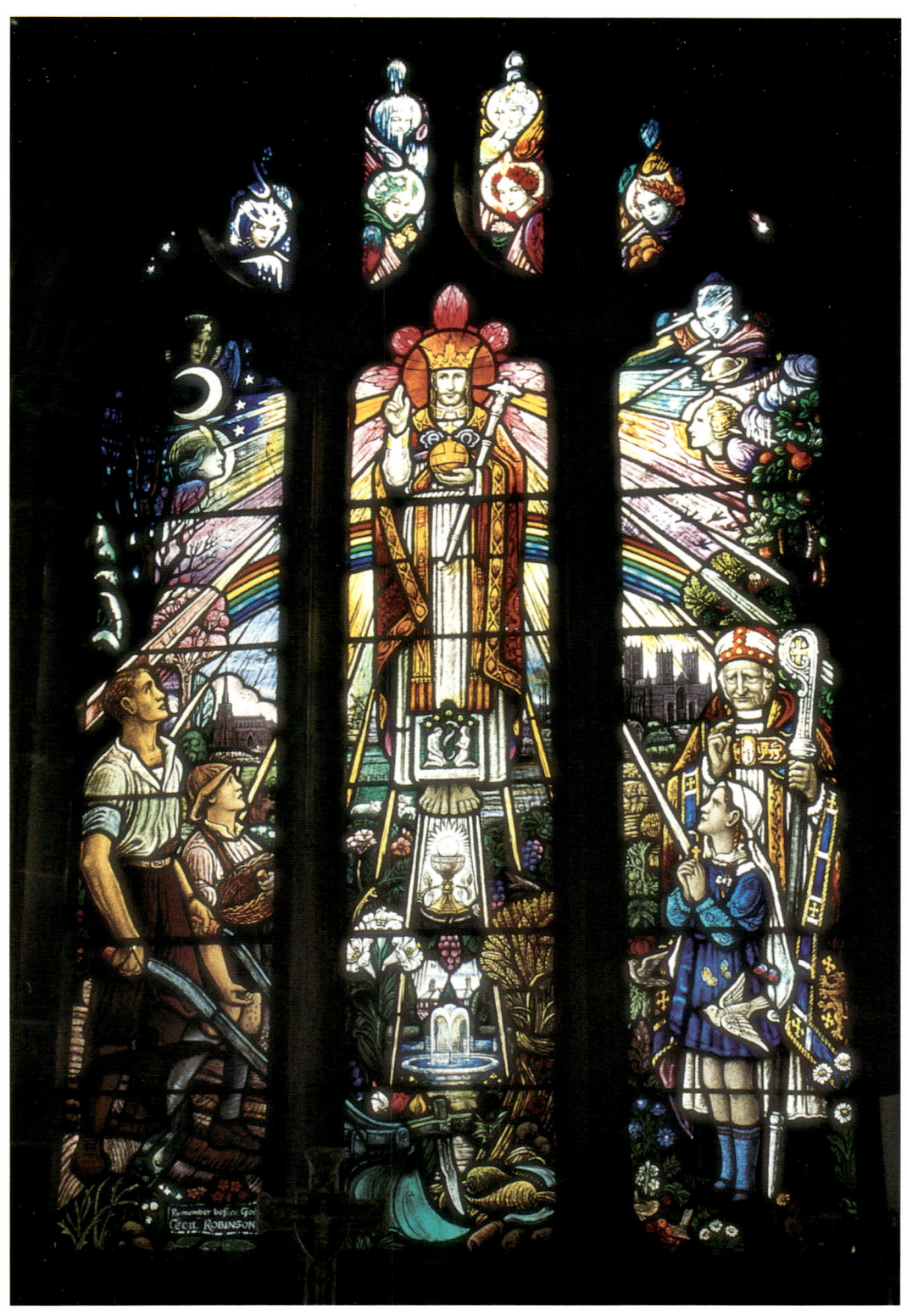

16. Quadring, St Margaret, *Christ in Majesty (The Seasons)*, 1945.

17. Wrangle, St Mary and St Nicholas, *The Incarnation, St Hugh and St Nicholas,* 1949, design.

18. Wrangle, St Mary and St Nicholas**,** *The Incarnation, St Hugh and St Nicholas* 1949, detail of cartoon.

19. Wrangle, St Mary and St Nicholas, *The Incarnation, St Hugh and St Nicholas*, 1949.

20. Sedgley, Dudley, St Mary, *St Christopher*, 1949.

21. Lye, Stourbridge, Christ Church, *World War II Memorial*, 1951.

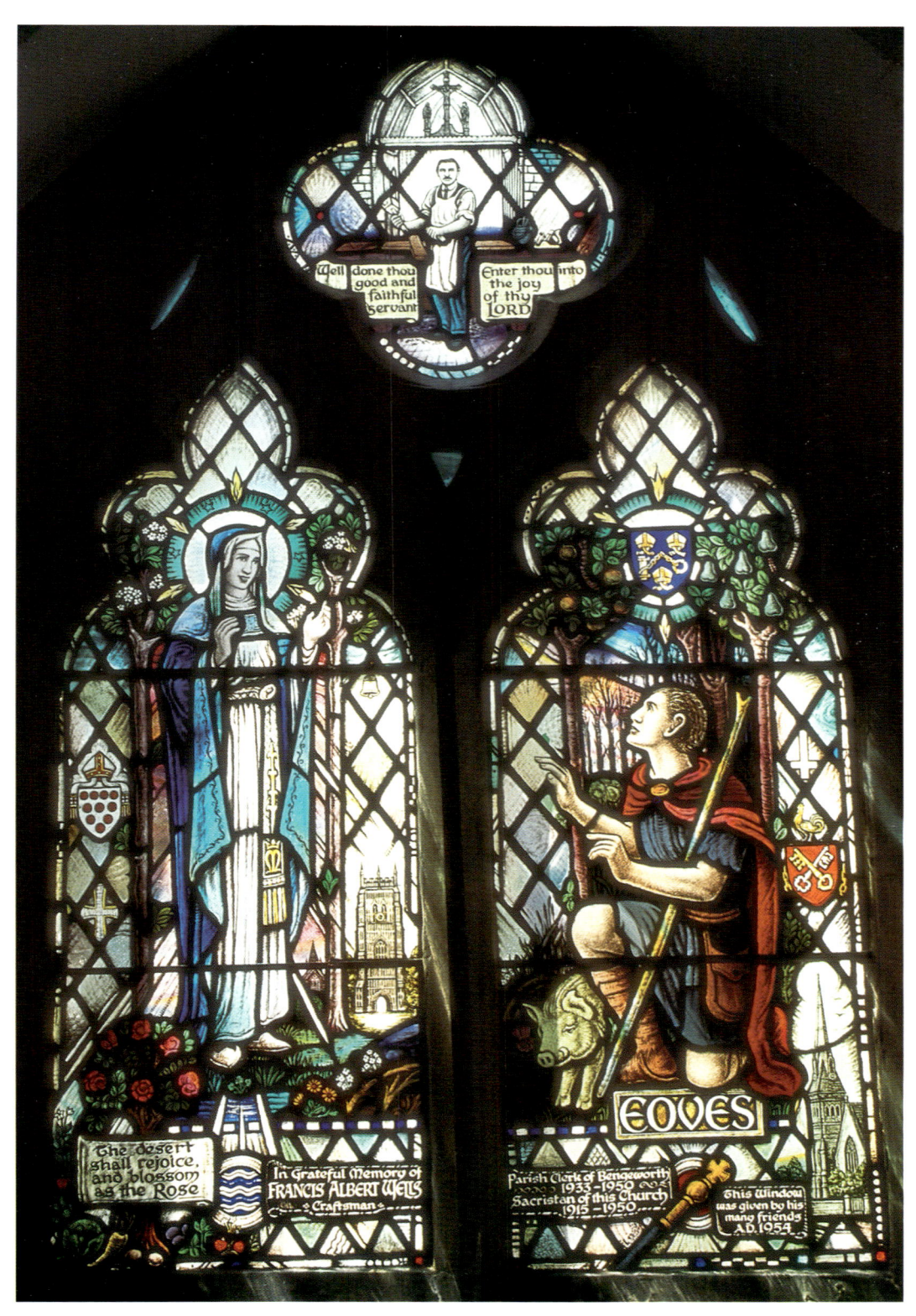

22. Evesham, Bengeworth, St Peter, *Eoves' Vision*, 1954.

23. Bromsgrove, St John, *Boy Scout*, c. 1955 (detail).

24. Taradale, New Zealand, All Saints, cartoon for *Trinity* window, 1956, (detail).

25. Bromsgrove, Catshill, Christ Church, *St Chad*, 1958.

26. Altar Cross, Gesso, paint and gold leaf on wood, date unknown, privately owned.

27. Portrait of Peter Lemmon, enamel, 1926, privately owned.

A.E. & P.E. Lemmon
Bromsgrove

Gazetteer of Stained Glass Windows

Entries are arranged in the following order:

Town, County
Church or chapel dedication, or other building.
Position in building, number of lights, date.
Subject depicted.
To whom dedicated with date of death, where known.
Donor with relationship, where known.
Signature – (AEL) Albert Lemmon, (PEL) Peter Lemmon, (DCT) Miss D C Turner.

*Indicates other art works by Lemmon.

Anwick, Lincolnshire.
St Edith.

Nave, south aisle, east wall, three lights and tracery, 1947.
Our Lady of Lincoln with St Edith and St George (World War II memorial).
Memorial to all men and women who served in the Second World War and all those who gave their lives, especially Charles Geoffrey Newton and Reginald Holland.
Donated by parishioners.
AEL and PEL.

Nave, north aisle, east window, three lights and tracery, 1952.
Christ with animals and birds in a landscape.
800th Anniversary window.
Donated by the Congregation.
AEL and PEL.

Birmingham, Aston.
All Souls.

East window, four lights and tracery, 1933.
Spirit of Birmingham.
Twenty-fifth anniversary of the consecration of the Church.
Donated by parishioners.

Nave, south wall, two lights, c. 1948.
Home Life of Our Lord.
George Hopkins, 28 July 1947, and Mary Ellen Hopkins his wife.

All Souls Church made redundant in 1981 and is now occupied by the Church of God (Universal).

Birmingham, Balsall Heath.
St Paul.

Chancel, north wall, lancet, c. 1936.
St Paul.
Alice Williams and her daughter.
Donor unknown.

Window relocated to the new St Paul's Church. It is framed and hangs in the north chancel.

Birmingham.
Children's Hospital.

Two lights.
St Barnabus and St Nicholas.

Window destroyed in World War II.

Birmingham, Ladywood.
St Margaret.

Single light, baptistery, faculty 8 November 1911.
Christ Blessing Children.
Revd Arthur Orlando Cherrington.
Donor unknown.

Church made redundant in 1956 and demolished.

Birmingham, Stirchley.
The Ascension.

South west clerestory, lancet, c. 1947.
St Anne Teaching the Virgin.
Lucy Harris, 12 June 1946.
Husband and children.

Relocated to new church (consecrated 14 July 1973) after the original church was damaged by fire.

*Bishopstone, Herefordshire
St Lawrence

Resetting of seven medieval and later panels, 1954
Chancel, south window, two lights and tracery
The panels are thought to have been collected by The Revd Lane Freer and assembled here in 1842. In 1954 Lemmon restored the window and identified the seven panels as dating from c. 1500 to c. 1840.

*Bromsgrove, Worcestershire.
All Saints.

South transept, south wall, two lights and tracery, 1927.
The Annunciation and St George (Plates 5, 6 and cover).
Aneurin Weber Evans, 30 September 1917, and Doris Mable Evans, 5 January 1926.
Donated by the Brighton family (Doris Mable Evans nee Brighton).
AEL and DCT.

Nave, south wall, two lights and tracery, 1932.
The Magnificat.
Elizabeth Kings, 9 October 1931.
Husband and children.
AEL and DCT.

Vestry, south wall, two lights.

St Wulstan, St Augustine and Prayers.
Donor unknown.

Vicar's Vestry, east wall, two lights.
Heraldic Arms of Worcester Diocese and All Saints Church with All Saints Church Prayer.
Donor unknown.

Bromsgrove, Worcestershire.
Bromsgrove School, Housman Hall of Residence(formerly Perry Hall Hotel, previously the home of A E Housman).

Entrance Hall, two rectangular panels, c. 1949.
Medieval Bromsgrove.
Donor unknown.
AEL.

Bromsgrove, Worcestershire.
Methodist Church.

North wall, lancet, c. 1957.
St Cecilia.
Harry Irish, 2 August 1956.
Wife.

This window was modified and relocated from the former Bromsgrove Methodist Church to this new building in 1983.

Bromsgrove, Worcestershire.
Bromsgrove Museum.

Two examples of the work of the Lemmon studio.
1. **St Christopher, c.1953.**
2. **St Aiden, c. 1953.**

These form part of a display, including design sketches and other items by A E Lemmon, loaned to the Museum by Peter Lemmon.

Bromsgrove, Worcestershire.
Rock Hill (Private House).

Four windows with leaded lights containing small pieces of coloured glass in a house built for Albert Lemmon's sister, Anne Isabel, and her husband Frederick Frost.

Bromsgrove, Worcestershire.
St John.

South porch, west wall, two lights and tracery, 1958.
Boy Scout window (Plate 23).
Douglas Ruxton Berwick, 24 October 1954.
Donated by his mother.
PEL.

*Bromsgrove, Worcestershire.
St Peter RC.

Nave, south wall, three lights and tracery, 1942.
St Peter the Fisherman.
Hanson family.
Harriet Mary Ann Hanson.
AEL.

*Bromsgrove, Catshill, Worcestershire.
Christ Church.

Nave, south wall, lancet, 1958.
St Chad (Plate 25).
Dorothy Irene Griffin, 17 May 1957, Edward Roy Griffin, 18 September 1955.
Mr and Mrs R E Griffin (parents).
PEL.

*Bromsgrove, Finstall, Worcestershire.
St Godwald.

1. South transept, south wall, two lights and tracery, and two side lancets, 1937.
Annunciation, St Barbara and St Cecilia.
Barbara Ethel Palmer, 7 December 1936.
Donated by her parents.

2. Nave, south wall, two lights and tracery, 1964.
St Gregory and St Anne.
John Busk, 12 July 1954, and Emily Eliza Busk, 24 October 1961.
Donated by their children.
Designed and begun by AEL, completed by PEL assisted by Arthur Clarke.
AEL and PEL.

Evesham, Bengeworth, Worcestershire.
St Peter.

1. Nave, north wall, two lights and tracery, 1937.
Christ in Joseph's Workshop.
John Hopkins.
Donated by his friends.
AEL.

2. Nave, south wall, two lights and tracery, 1938.
Good Shepherd and Good Samaritan.
Thomas and Sarah Selina Bedenham.
Annie Selina Urmston (daughter).
AEL.

3. Nave, south wall, two lights and tracery, 1954.
Eoves' Vision (Plate 22).
Frances Albert Wells.
Donated by his friends.
AEL and PEL.

Halesowen, West Midlands.
St Margaret.

East window, five lights and tracery, 1935.
Christ with St Margaret, St Mary Virgin, St John the Baptist and St Kenelm (Plate 10).
John Small, Noah and Jane Fellows.
Charlotte Small, (wife) nee Fellows (daughter).
AEL

*Helpringham, Lincolnshire.
St Andrew.

Nave, north aisle, east wall, three lights and tracery, 1940.
Christ in Majesty with St Hugh of Lincoln and St Andrew (Plate 12).
Robert Knowles Watts.
Susannah Kate Watts (wife).
AEL.

Nave, north wall, three lights and tracery, 1943.
St Luke, St Gilbert and Bishop Edward of Lincoln.
Cecil Robinson and Tom Arthur White.
Donated by Edward E Robinson.
AEL and PEL.

Nave, south aisle, south wall, three lights and tracery, 1946.
Seven Sacraments.
Henry Hine Foster, Duncan McInnes, George Raynard Lee, Harold William Dods, James Gordon Jeudwine, Joseph Gladstone Robinson, Alfred Willis White, Norman Snow, William Shuckburgh Swane – Bishop, Earnest Julius Turkhian – Priest, Edmund John Stephens – priest, Walter Hicks – Canon, Alfred Hunt – Canon, Basil Gordon Nicholas – Canon, Joseph James Swann –Priest, Foster Ashwin – Priest.
Donated by Edward E Robinson.
AEL and PEL.

Nave, south wall, three lights, 1950.
St Christopher, St Faith and St Edward of England.
Joseph and Fanny Taylor, George Martin (verger) and all travellers by land, sea and air.
Donated by Edward E Robinson.

West window (tower), three lights and tracery, 1950.
Bishop Robert Grossetesta, St Lawrence and The Venerable Bede.
John Athelston Lawie Riley (Patron) and all Bishops, Priests and Deacons who have served the needs of this parish.
Donated by Edward E Robinson.

Little Witley, Worcestershire.
St Michael and All Angels.

West window, two lights and tracery, 1953.
St Michael.
Donated by the Friends of St Michael's Church.
AEL.

*Lye, Stourbridge, West Midlands.
Christ Church.

1. South transept, east wall, two lights and tracery, 1951.
Christ administering Holy Communion to Armed Forces (Plate 21).
World War II Memorial (49 names).
Donated by Parishioners.
AEL and PEL.

2. North transept, east wall, lancet, 1951.
Good Shepherd.
The Rev William Smart.
Donated by parishioners.
AEL and PEL.

The north transept has been reordered to create lower and upper rooms. The floor of the upper room bisects this window.

3. Nave, south wall, single light, 1952.
St Andrew.
Donated by Thomas Henry Hodgkiss.
AEL and PEL.

4. South transept, west wall, two lights and tracery, 1952.
Clear rectangular quarries with small area of blue glass in heads of main lights and tracery.

Metheringham, Lincolnshire.
St Wilfrid.

Nave, south wall, three lights and tracery, 1947.
Virgin and Child, St Elizabeth and St Joseph.
John William and Emma Beal Skins.
Helena (daughter).
AEL and PEL.

*Quadring, Lincolnshire.
St Margaret.

North aisle, east wall, three lights and tracery, 1945.
Christ in Majesty and the seasons (Plate 16).
Cecil Robinson.
Brothers and Sisters of C Robinson.
AEL and PEL.

Nave, north wall, three lights and tracery, 1953.
Crucifixion.
Donated by the Robinson family.

Nave, north wall, three lights and tracery, 1953.
Christ among the Elders.
Donated by the Robinson family.
AEL and PEL.

Nave, north wall, three lights and tracery, 1953.
Presentation in the Temple.
Donated by the Robinson family.

Rowney Green, Worcestershire.
Shared Church (Methodist).

East window, round, 1951.
Christ Blessing Children.
Caroline Quinney.
E G Quinney (husband) and family.

*Sedgley, Dudley, West Midlands.

St Mary the Virgin.

Nave, south wall, lancet, 1947.
St Francis.
David Hughes Hartland, 29 March 1943.
Mrs M Hartland (wife).

Nave, south wall, lancet, 1948.
St Elizabeth and St John the Baptist.
David Hughes Hartland, 29 March 1943.
Mrs M Hartland (wife) and daughters Mrs Vera Nancy Price and Mrs Kathleen Mary Pincher.
AEL and PEL.

Nave, south wall, lancet, 1949.
St Christopher (Plate 20).
Arthur Howes.
Mrs Howes (wife).

Nave, south wall, lancet, 1952.
Holy Family.
Joseph and Harriet Nicholls.
Donated by their sons.
AEL and PEL.

Nave, south wall, lancet, 1962.
St Gregory.
Thomas William Hughes Meddings.
Dora Irene Meddings (wife).
PEL.

Sheffield

Location unknown.

Two lights and tracery.
Christ blessing children and St George.

Silian, Lampeter, Ceredigion

St Sulian.

East window, three lights, 1936.
Christ, St Mary and St David (Plate 11).
John Stewart, 1919, Margaret Stewart (wife) 1928, Jenkin William Stewart (son) 1921.
Donated by the children of John and Margaret Stewart.

Taradale, New Zealand.

All Saints.

East window, three lights, 1956.
Trinity (Plate 24 and Frontispiece).
George Frank Lemmon, 1949.
Elsie Edith Lemmon (wife).
AEL and PEL.

Nave, south wall, single light, 1960.
St Andrew.
The Anderson family.
Donated by Waldo Anderson.

Nave, south wall, single light, 1960.
St Cecilia.
The Anderson family.
Donated by Waldo Anderson.
PEL.

*Thornborough, Buckinghamshire.

St Mary.

Chancel, north wall, two lights and tracery, 1944.
Christ in Joseph's Workshop (Plate 14).
The Rev. William Richard Williams.
Donated by the congregation.
AEL and PEL.

Tividale, Dudley, West Midlands.

St Michael.

1941.
St Elizabeth and St John the Baptist.
Harriet Annie Edwards, 15 April 1939.
William Hugh Wright Edwards (husband).

The original church of St Michael was demolished c. 1981 but this window was not relocated in the new St Michael's Church. The present location of the window is not known.

West Bromwich, West Midlands.

Christ Church.

Three lights, 1928.
St Aiden, St Augustine, and St Chad (Plate 8).
Maria Wakeman.
Legacy of Mary Ann Wakeman (daughter).

Three lights and tracery.
Christ in Majesty.

The final service was held at Christ Church in 1975 and the church demolished in 1980. The present location of windows is not known.

West Bromwich, Greets Green, West Midlands.

St Peter.

East window, four lights and tracery, 1930.
Christ in Majesty – Te Deum (Plate 9).
Donated by parishioners.
AEL.

Nave, north wall, three lights and tracery, 1939.
Resurrection and Disciples at the Empty Tomb.
Samuel Pearson, 4 January 1938.
Lydia Pearson (wife) and children.
AEL and PEL.

Nave, south wall, three lights ands tracery, 1943.
Christ calling St Andrew and St Peter.
Charles Lucas, 9 January 1940.
Donated by his wife.
AEL.

Wolverhampton, West Midlands.
St George.

1. Nave, north wall, round-headed, 1928.
Holy Family with St Elizabeth and St Anne.
Adela Maud Hill, 16 December 1926.
J T Hill (husband).

2. Nave, north wall, round-headed, 1928.
The Communion of Saints.
The Revd John Henry Hamilton.
Congregation and friends.

3. Nave, north wall, round-headed. 1933.
Ascension.
Frederick William Bradford, 10 January 1931.
Madge Bradford (wife), and Frederick John Bradford (son) and Mrs Mary Lowe (daughter).

Church demolished. Present location of the windows unknown.

Wrangle, Lincolnshire.
St Mary and St Nicholas.

Nave, south aisle, east wall, four lights and tracery, 1949.
The Incarnation, St Hugh of Lincoln and St Nicholas (Plates 17, 18 and 19).
George Walter Wood.
Lucy Wood (wife).
AEL and PEL.

Unknown Location.

Single light.
St George and the Dragon.
Known from the cartoon.

Two light.
Christ Blessing Children and St George.
Known from photographs of the design and the cartoon, annotated 'Cartoon and Colour Sketch for Window (Sheffield)'.

Gazetteer of Decorative Art Works

Items are listed according to location, in alphabetical order, except for those which are privately owned which are recorded at the end of the gazetteer.

Town, County.
Church dedication.
Object, medium and date.
Brief description.
To whom dedicated, with date of death, where known.
Donor, where known.

*Indicates stained glass by Lemmon at the same location.

*Anwick, Lincolnshire.
St Edith.

Two carved, painted, wooden angels.
The angels embellish the oak panelling on the east and north walls of the Children's corner in the north-east nave could be the work of A E Lemmon.

Churchwardens' Staves.
The Royal Crown and the Bishop's Crown heads of the Churchwardens' staves, in gesso and paint on wood, probably by Lemmon.

Birmingham, Edgbaston.
St James.

Reredos.
Located in the north transept this reredos was referred to in a Birmingham Diocesan document of 1970. St James' Church was made redundant and sold in 1976. Details and present location of the reredos are unknown.

Birmingham, Erdington.
Highcroft Hospital (Erdington House) Chapel.

Altar front, painted panels on oak.
Depicted on the five painted panels are an Angel, St Mary kneeling, standing Christ holding a chalice, St John kneeling and an Angel.
Tester Beam.
Memorial panels, painted wood, west wall.

Highcroft Hospital has been demolished and the site redeveloped.

Birmingham, Small Heath.
St Gregory.

Reredos, paint and gesso on wood.
St Gregory Mass in Blessed Sacrament Chapel (north).

Reredos, paint and gesso on wood in Chapel of Our Lady (south).
The Communion of Our Lady (Autumn).
Children's Shrine.
Painted panel depicting St Joseph with the Boy Jesus.
Painted rectangular mural panels.
1. The Annunciation (Spring).
2. The Visitation (Summer).
3. The Nativity (Winter).

St Gregory's Church was declared redundant in 1995 and sold to the Bethel United Church in 1996. The present location of the above works is unknown.

*Bishopstone, Herefordshire.
St Lawrence.

Renovation of the reredos and panelling in the chancel. The reredos is of carved oak thought to be from the sixteenth century, with additional later carving and panelling.
Refurbished with a donation from the Lewis family, 1954

*Bromsgrove, Worcestershire.
All Saints.

Churchwarden staves, wood with gesso, paint and gold leaf, 1931 (Plate 7).
The Parish Warden's stave has the arms of the Diocese of Worcester and on the reverse Royal Arms.
The Vicar's Warden's stave has the badge of All Saints Church and on the reverse a shield depicting various religious symbols with Christ in majesty above.
Gift of A E Lemmon.

Church Verge (Mace), wood, gesso, paint, gold and silver leaf.
Each side has figures and heraldic arms depicted with an embattled castle with spire, representing the church, at the top. The west side has a figure of St John the Baptist and the arms of St Augustine, St Michael and the crest of Bromsgrove. The east side has a figure of Our Lady and the arms of St Benedict and St Nicholas. On the south side are the arms of Canterbury, The Dean of Worcester, St Wulstan and St Richard de Wyche. The north side has the arms of St Andrew, St Chad and St Kenelm.
Gift of A E Lemmon.

Painted Reredos and Riddel Posts, 1933.
The Holy Family with St Anne, St Elizabeth and St John the Baptist, depicted on the wooden reredos, in gesso, paint and gold leaf. The riddel posts surmounted by carved painted angel candlesticks, which are now in another part of the building.

Reredos and posts, part-painted wood
Half-panelled oak reredos with a painted statue of Christ as a child in a niche, beneath an architectural canopy, and a painted angel baptising a child at a font in gesso and paint, and a painted inscription 'INCREASED IN WISDOM AND STATURE AND IN FAVOUR WITH GOD AND MAN'. Four, pine, painted, altar posts capped with candleholders.

Patronal Banner, painted fabric.
Depicts a standing figure of the Christ-Child with birds, butterflies and flowers and the inscription 'OUR LORD OUR BROTHER'. At the bottom is the badge of All Saints Church (Sanctus, Sanctus, Sanctus and a crown). Signed AEL.

Processional Banner of Guild of Servants of the Sanctuary in painted fabric, 1941
The banner depicts St Kenelm after whom the Bromsgrove Chapter of the Guild is named.
It is in memory of Fred Roberson, aged 22, a chapter member who died at Dunkirk in May 1940. Signed by Bernard Roberson, brother of Fred, who was also a member of the chapter, the banner was made at Bromsgrove Art School where Bernard was a student. The style and iconography show the influence, and perhaps the hand, of A E Lemmon who was art teacher at the time. The banner was consecrated on 19 April 1941.

*Bromsgrove, Worcestershire.
St Peter.

Painted Shrine, gesso, tempera and gold leaf, 1936.
Blessed Martyrs Shrine triptych depicting Christ the King, St John Fisher and St Thomas More.
Donated by Albert Lemmon and his sister Ann Frost, and William Moore.

Painted panel, 1943.
Blessed John Wall.

Painted panel.
St Theresa.

Illuminated Page, 1947.
Dedicatory page of Altar Missal presented to Father W E Warner.

Bromsgrove, Worcestershire.
Watt Close School.

'Heraldic Arms' of the School, paint and gesso on a wooden cut-out panel.

This former Secondary Modern School building is now St John's CE Middle School. The present location of the shield is unknown.

*Bromsgrove, Catshill, Worcestershire.
Christ Church.

Processional Cross, gesso and paint on wood, c. 1929.
A St Chad's cross with 'Jesus' and a chalice and host, wheat and grapes in a mandorla in the centre. Also depicted are the arms of Worcester Diocese and 'Chadshill' against a setting sun.

*Bromsgrove, Finstall, Worcestershire.
St Godwald.

Patronal banner, painted fabric, 1927.
Banner depicts St Godwald in Bishop's vestments, scroll with inscription 'Sanctus Godwald Patronus' and New Testament and local scenes.

*Helpringham, Lincolnshire.
St Andrew.

Chapel of St Hugh, nave, north aisle, east end, 1940.

Wooden triptych, gesso and paint (Plate 13).
The open triptych depicts the Resurrected Christ above a kneeling angel at the empty tomb, two disciples to the left and two Marys to the right. When closed the altarpiece shows Christ's Agony in the Garden.

Altar candlesticks (pair), gesso and paint on wood.

Painted wooden, cut-out panel.
St Hugh preaching.

Aumbry door, gesso and paint on wood.
Embellished with the Pelican in her Piety in a mandorla and swan hinges.

Donated in memory of Robert Knowles Watts by his wife, Susannah Kate Watts, in 1940.

Nave, south aisle, east end, Lady Chapel (Armed Forces Chapel), 1947.

East wall.

Altar cross and candlesticks, gesso and paint on wood.
The cross depicts Christ in Majesty.
In memory of Ernest Jim Foremen.

Four painted wooden candlesticks.
Two are freestanding and two mounted on corbels. They support carved, painted figures of saints representing the armed forces – St Nicholas, St George, St Michael and St Andrew. The free-standing candlesticks supporting St Nicholas (Royal Navy) and St George (Army) are in memory of Albert Robinson and were donated by his parents and brothers and sisters. The corbel-mounted candlesticks, St Michael (RAF) and St Andrew (Royal Navy), are in memory of Charles Christian Bird and were the gift of his mother.

Altar Rail, forces badges painted on wood.
The wooden rail supporting the altar curtain has small painted badges of women's services – Womens' Land Army, British Red Cross, Women's Transport Service and Auxiliary Territorial Service, with a WREN and a WRAF kneeling holding a shield bearing a lily in a vase.

Forces badges, cut-outs in wood with gesso and painted decoration.
Three painted badges representing the Royal Navy, the Army and the Royal Air Force.

Aumbry Door.

Chancel, east end, main altar.

Decoration of the altar, gesso and paint on wood.
The front of this oak altar is embellished with attached painted panels depicting St Andrew standing in a sailing boat, lily, rose, thistle, shamrock, leeks, and badges of the church and diocese.

*Lye, Stourbridge, West Midlands.
Christ Church.

Altar candlesticks, gesso and paint on wood, 1951.
A pair of candlesticks with circular bases.

A letter at Worcester Record Office written by Lemmon seem to indicate that these candlesticks were part of a group of objects designed by him as part of a War Memorial, including his stained glass window. Other elements of the proposed memorial included an oak altar, two posts and cornice in softwood, decorated with gesso and paint, and an altar cross also decorated with gesso and painted. Perhaps only the candlesticks were made.

*Quadring, Lincolnshire.
St Margaret.

Nave, north aisle, east wall (Lady Chapel) 1953.

Altar front, gesso and painted images.
Three panels depicting the Annunciation, left the Virgin kneeling, central panel the Holy Dove in a circle the colours of the rainbow, right panel St Gabriel.

Altar cross and candlesticks, gesso and paint on wood.
Crucified Christ depicted on the altar cross.

Aumbry door.
The door is embellished with a painted wooden cut-out of St Mary and the Christ-Child and painted lion-head hinges. Above the door is a painted cut-out of two kneeling angels.

The above items were donated in memory of Cecil Robinson in 1953.

Painted, wooden, cut-out panels on oak panelling with posts, 1963.
Three painted cut-out panels. St Bernard (signed AEL and PEL 1963) and St Margaret on painted panels attached to the panelling. The painted cut-out of St Cecilia (signed and dated) is free-standing. There are six posts which support candle-holders.

St Michael South Elham, Suffolk.
St Michael and All Angels.

Reredos, three panels, painted wood.
St Michael, St Felix and St Fursey.

*Sedgley, West Midlands.
St Mary.

Painted statue and candlesticks, 1954.
Painted plaster statue of standing St Mary holding Christ-Child, and a pair of painted wooden candlesticks on a painted wooden shelf.
In memory of David Hughes Hartland.
Donated by Mrs M Hartland and her daughters.

Sutton Coldfield, Wylde Green, West Midlands
Emmanuel Church.

Rood Screen, 1927, figures repainted by Lemmon in 1953.
Carved wooden figures in the round of Christ crucified, St Mary and St John by R L Boulton & Sons, Cheltenham, repainted by Lemmon.
Donated by Harold and Madge Simpson in memory of their brothers Leslie and Reginald Burdge who fell in the Great War.

*Thornborough, Buckinghamshire.
St Mary.

Altarpiece, gesso and paint on wood, 1946.
Three separate painted panels, centre panel has standing figure of Christ, left panel a seated mother with two children beneath St Mary the mother of Jesus and the third panel depicts a kneeling Royal Marine beneath St Martin.
Martin Christopher Brown, 22 May 1941.
Donated by his father and mother.

Candlesticks, gesso and paint on wood, 1946.
Two painted wooden altar candlesticks.

Sanctuary Screen, Beam and Rood, gesso and paint on wood, 1946.
The screen is three sections of low oak panelling between four posts with painted decoration. The centre section is a pair of doors opening into the Sanctuary. The screen was donated by men and women who served in Second World War, in thanks for their safe return, and in tribute to fallen comrades.

Sanctuary screen with rood (Plate 15).
The sanctuary beam, with emblems of the armed forces, supports a Rood of painted cut-out panels of the Crucifixion, St Mary and St John.
Cyril Frank Capel, 23 June 1943.
Donated by his family.

Roll of Honour 1939-1945, painted wood, 1946.
Painted oak board bearing the name, rank and service of forty-seven villagers who served in the forces. The names of those who did not return are indicated with the word 'obit' and brief details of where and when they died.

*Wolverhampton, West Midlands.
St George.

Memorial, paint and gesso on wood, c. 1932.
Wall-mounted memorial depicting St Michael holding a child.
Donated by The Revd Charles Dearnley in memory of his son Michael Dearnley, 30 December 1931.

Church demolished. Present location of the memorial unknown.

Worcester.
Worcestershire Records Office.

Worcestershire Regiment Cap-Badges, drawings on paper, c. 1944.
Photocopies of five imperial size (762 x 559 mm) sheets of paper with drawings and associated text outlining the history of the Worcestershire Regiment through its cap-badges from 1649. Four of the five are signed AEL.
The drawings were deposited at the Record Office in 1951, by Major W V Watton, having previously been in the custody of Bromsgrove Home Guard.

Privately owned items.

Enamel, 1926? (Plate 27).
A small enamel on metal depicting Peter Lemmon, aged 6, head and shoulders in profile, with the inscription 'PETER 1926'.

Altar Cross, gesso and paint on wood (Plate 26).
Christ in majesty and crucified Christ. Height 1060 mm.

Altar Cross, gesso and paint on wood.
Christ on the cross with St Mary and St John. Two monks stand at the base of the cross. Height 540 mm.

Candlesticks, gesso and paint on wood.
A pair of painted altar candlesticks with small shields with lilies in a vase and a pierced heart. Height 480 mm.

Candlesticks, gesso and paint on wood.
A pair of painted wooden candlesticks with painted lily and pelican in her piety and lily and phoenix. Height 600 mm.

Unknown Location.

Carved wooden heraldic arms
– probably painted, or repainted, by AEL. Motto 'LOYAL DEVIOR'.

Bibliography

Albutt, Roy, *Stained Glass Windows of Bromsgrove and Redditch, Worcestershire,* (Pershore: Roy Albutt, 2002)

Albutt, Roy, *The Stained Glass of A J Davies of the Bromsgrove Guild,* (Pershore: Roy Albutt, 2005).

Alexander, Jenny, *Angels and Oranges, Stained Glass Windows in the Churches of North Kesteven,* (North Kesteven District Council, 1996).

Anon, *St Lawrence Church Bishopstone Visitors Guide,* [n. d.].

Birmingham Museum and Art Gallery Sound Archive, *E Whitford and N Yoxall,* transcript of interview taped 12 August 1983.

Birmingham Museum and Art Gallery Sound Archive, *Arthur Slade Clarke,* transcript of interview taped 11 April 1984.

Briggs, Jonathan, 'The Watermills of Bromsgrove', in Foster, John, ed., *Bygone Bromsgrove* (Bromsgrove: Bromsgrove Society, 1981).

Broderick, A G, 'A Memory of Mr Lemmon', in *Bromsgrove Society Newsletter,* Volume 25, Number 3, (September 2005), pp. 2-3.

Chinn, Carl, *Homes for People: Council Housing and Urban Renewal in Birmingham, 1849-1999,* (Studley: Brewin Books, 1999).

Cormack, Peter, *The Stained Galss Work of Christopher Whall 1849-1924* (USA: Boston Library, 1999).

Donnelly, Michael, *Scotland's Stained Glass: Making the Colours Sing,* (Edinburgh: The Stationery Office, 1997).

French, Sonia and Tom, 'The Patronal Banner of St Godwald', in *St Godwald's Parish Magazine,* (October 2006), pp. 16-19.

Goodwin, Marlene and Townshend, Jenny, 'The Workers at the Bromsgrove Guild', in Watt, Quintin, ed., *The Bromsgrove Guild An Illustrated History* (Bromsgrove: Bromsgrove Society, 1999).

Grierson, Janet, *St Godwald's: A Parish and It's People*, (Bromsgrove: St Godwald's Parochial Church Council, 1984).

Hartnell, Roy, *Pre-Raphaelite Birmingham,* (Studley: Brewin Books, 1996).

Honey, Thomas M, *Stained Glass Windows of Gordon Webster,* (Bristol: Morris and Juliet Venables, 2002).

Kings, Bill, *Old Rover Selections from the Cartoons of Arthur Clarke,* (Bromsgrove: Silly Symbol Productions, 1993).

Lemmon, Albert Edward, *Yuletide Greetings from the 5th Battalion Cameron Highlanders,* (Glasgow: MacLure, McDonald & Co, 1919).

McCardel, James, *New Kilpatrick Parish and It's Story,* (Glasgow: Bell and Bain, 1973).

McKenna, Joseph, *Birmingham The Building of a City,* (Stroud: Tempus, 2005).

Newbold, John, *A History of the Catholic Church in Bromsgrove,* (Bromsgrove: Chris Floate, 1992).

Pevsner, Nikolaus, *Industrial Art in England,* (Cambridge: CUP, 1937).

Pugh, John, *Bromsgrove and the Housmans,* (Bromsgrove: The Housman Society, 1974).

Swift, John, *Changing Fortunes: the Birmingham School of Art Building 1880-1995,* (Birmingham: Article Press, 1996).

Townshend, Jenny, 'A Tale of Two Pubs' in *The Bromsgrove Rousler*, Vol. 20, (December 2005), pp. 15-21.

Watt, Quentin, ed., *The Bromsgrove Guild, An Illustrated History* (Bromsgrove: Bromsgrove Society, 1999).

Index

Adam, Stephen 7, 8, 11
Alston Street, Ladywood 4
Alvechurch, Rowney Green, Shared Church 24, 75
Anwick, Lincolnshire, St Edith 33-34, 67, 81
Aston, Birmingham, Church of God 25-26, 68
Arts and Crafts Movement 6, 39
Balsall Heath, Birmingham, St Paul 26, 68
Bengeworth, Evesham, St Peter 24, 36, 72, Plate 22
Birmingham and Midland Institute 17
Birmingham, Aston, Church of God 25-26, 68
    Balsall Heath, St Paul 26
    Children's Hospital Chapel (former) 29, 68
    Edgbaston, St James 30, 82
    Erdington, Highcroft Hall, Hospital Chapel 30, 82
    Ladywood, Alston Street 4
        Great Tindal Street 2, 4
        St Margaret 5, 25, 68
    Royal Society of Artists 18
    St Chad's Cathedral 5
    St Philip's Cathedral
    School of Art 4, 5-7, Plate 1
    Small Heath, St Gregory 30, 82
    Stirchley, The Ascension 69
Bishopstone, Herefordshire, St Lawrence 37, 69, 83
Bourne, Swaine, 4, 8 note 3
Bradford Cathedral 12
Bromsgrove, All Saints 3, 11, 20-22, 69-70, 83-84, Plates 5, 6, 7 and cover
    Catshill, Christ Church 18, 71, 85, Plate 25
    Finstall, St Godwald 22, 72, 85
    Guild of Applied Arts 7, 9-10, 12
    Museum 70

       Methodist Church 23, 70
       St John 10, 18, 71, Plate 23
       St Peter 22-23, 71, 84
       School of Art 17, 22
       School 23, 38 note 6, 70
       Watt Close Secondary School (former) 84
Burne-Jones, Edward (1833-98) 5, 6
Camm, Florence (1874-1960) 7, 38 note 9
Camm T W & Co 4, 7, 8 note 3, 26, 38 note 9
Catshill, Bromsgrove, Christ Church 18, 71, 85, Plate 25

Chance Bros, Smethwick 16
Chew and Commander 16, 19 note 7
Children's Hospital Chapel (former) Birmingham 29, 68
Churchill, Worcestershire, St James 12
Clarke, Arthur Slade (1893-1993) 10, 12, 18
Davies, Archibald John (1877-1953) 7, 9, 10, 12, 20
Department of Science and Art 7
Edinburgh, Belford Hostel 12
Edgbaston, Birmingham, St James 30, 82
Erdington, Highcroft Hall Hospital Chapel, 30, 82
Evans, Samuel, 4, 5, 8 notes 3 and 4
Evesham, Bengeworth, St Peter 24, 36, 72, Plate 22
Finstall, Bromsgrove, St Godwald 22, 72, 85
Frost, Frederick (1872-1947) 22
Gilbert, Walter (1871-1946) 9
Great Tindal Street, Ladywood, Birmingham 2, 4
Greets Green, West Bromwich 27, 78-79, Plate 9
Guild of Applied Arts, Bromsgrove 7, 9-10, 12
Halesowen, Dudley, St Margaret 27, 73, Plate 10
Hardman Stained Glass Studios 1, 4, 5, 8 note 3, 15, 18
Hartley Wood & Co 16, 19 note 8
Hasbury, Halesowen, St Margaret, 27, 73, Plate 10
Helpringham, Lincolnshire, St Andrew 31-32, 73-74, 85-86, Plates 12 and 13
Highcroft Hall Hospital Chapel, Erdington 30, 82

Hodgetts, Henry John (1897-1964) 10, 12

Housman House, Bromsgrove School 23, 38 note 6, 70

Jones and Willis 4, 8 note 3

Ladywood, Birmingham, Alston Street 4
    Great Tindal Street 2, 4
    St Margaret 5, 25, 68

Lansdowne Church, Glasgow 7

Leaded Lights 1, 2

Lemmon, Albert Edward art teacher 17, assistants 16, awards 6-7, Birmingham School of Art 5-7, Bromsgrove Guild 9-10, 12, family 2, 4, 5, 11, 39, signatures 18, studio 15-17, First World War 3, 10-12, Second World War 17, Guild of Designer Craftsmen 17-18, Frontispiece, *Yuletide Greetings* 10-12, Plates 3 and 4

Lemmon, Anne Isabel (sister) 5, 22, 23

Lemmon, Elizabeth (sister) 4, 5

Lemmon, Frances Ellen (sister) 5

Lemmon, George Frank (brother) 5, 35, 77

Lemmon, Hilda (wife) nee Bridgman 2, 10-12, 20-21, 39, Plate 2

Lemmon, Peter Edward (son) 1, 3, 12, 15, 16, 18, 21, 22, 35, 39

Lemmon, Sarah (mother) nee Hodgetts 4

Lemmon, William (father) 4

Lemmon, William Henry (brother) 5, 10

Little Witley, Worcestershire, St Michael 24, 74

Lowndes and Drury, 6

Lye, Stourbridge, Christ Church 28-29, 74, 87, Plate 21

Machelli 17

Meredith, Alan 2, 16

Metheringham, Lincolnshire, St Wilfrid 34, 38 note 10, 75

Morris and Co 5

Morris, William (1834-96) 6

Newill, Mary (1860-1947) 9

New Kilpatrick Church, Bearsden, Strathclyde, 7

New Zealand see Taradale

Pancheri and Hack 14

Payne, Henry (1868-1940) 6, 7, 9

Pearce, William 4, 8 note 3

Perry Hall, Bromsgrove 23, 38 note 6, 70

Powell, James and Sons 16

Quadring, Lincolnshire, St Margaret 33, 75, 87, Plate 16

Roberson, Bernard 21, 22

Roberson, Frederick 21

Rowney Green, Alvechurch, Shared Church 24, 75

Rushbury, Henry George 7, 9

St Chad's Cathedral, Birmingham 5

St Michael South Elham, Suffolk, St Michael 88

St Philip's Cathedral, Birmingham 5

Sanders, Joseph Newbould (1885-1933) 7, 9, 13 note 4

Sedgley, Dudley, St Mary 18, 28, 76, 88, Plate 20

Silian, Ceredigion, St Sulian 36, 77, Plate 11

School of Art, Birmingham 4, 5-7, Plate 1

School of Art, Bromsgrove 17, 22

Sheffield 37, 76

Sleigh, Bernard (1872-1954) 9

Small Heath, Birmingham, St Gregory 30, 82

Stirchley, Birmingham, The Ascension 69

Stubington, Richard (1885-1966) 7

Sutton Coldfield, Wylde Green, Emmanuel Church 88

Taradale, New Zealand 18, 35, 77, Plate 24

Taylor, Edward 6

Thornborough, Buckinghamshire, St Mary 36, 77, 88, Plates 14 and 15

Tividale, Dudley, St Michael 78

Townsend Mill, Bromsgrove 10

Turner, Miss D C 16, 18

Watt Close Secondary School 84

Webster, Alfred Alexander (1884-1915) 7, 8, 11

Weingartner, Louis 11

West Bromwich, Christ Church 30, 78, Plate 8

West Bromwich, Greets Green, St Peter, 27, 78-79, Plate 9

Whall, Christopher 6

Wolverhampton, St George 30, 79, 89
    St Peter, 12

Worcestershire Guild of Designer Craftsmen 17, 18, 19 note 14
Worcestershire Records Office 89, Frontispiece
Wrangle, Lincolnshire, St Mary and St Nicholas 16, 34, 79, Plates 17, 18 and 19
Wylde Green, Sutton Coldfield, Emmanuel Church 88